Never Alone

How to survive the tough stuff life throws at you

Daniel Chuunga

First published in 2007
Copyright ©
All rights reserved. No part of this publication
may be reproduced in any form without prior
permission from the publisher.
Unless otherwise indicated, all Scripture quotations are taken
from the *New King James Version*.
British Library Cataloguing in Publication Data.
A catalogue record for this book is available
from the British Library.
ISBN 1-904685-40-4
Designed by Abigail Murphy
Published by The Stanborough Press Ltd., Grantham, England.
Printed in the USA

> Dear Shelley,
> Never Alone. Time and again through the difficult times in life, the promise in these words has reminded me that no matter what happens in this life, God is right there to help me through. Even though we go through those deep dark valley's, face seemingly insurmountable challenges and at times seem to be all alone, even then, He is right there with us. From personal experience I know this to be true. So I just wanted to let you know Shelley that we're still praying for you and that you're never alone.
> - Sarah

Never Alone

How to survive the tough stuff life throws at you

Daniel Chuunga

Never Alone

Contents

Acknowledgement 5
Dedication 5
Preface 5
Never Alone 6
Chastened, but not Forsaken 12
The Lord Was With Joseph 17
Under the Pillar of Cloud and Fire 23
Forty Years Feeding on One Dish 28
Water from the Rock in the Desert 32
Four Out of Three 36
When Enemies Plot 43
In the Valley of Death- I 51
In the Valley of Death- II 56
In Stormy Times 61
Look Up! 66
Do Not Fear 73
Never Give Up 80
Our Father 88
It is Over 93
Bibliography 106

Acknowledgement

I should like to express my profound gratitude to God the Father, the Son and the Holy Spirit for the gracious opportunity to enable me to bring this piece of work to completion. Further acknowledgements go to Pastor Victor Haangala for editorial assistance rendered.

Dedication

This book is dedicated to you, the reader. It is meant to encourage you to hold on to Jesus Christ who is able to give you peace in a world of trials.

Preface

This life is full of sorrows and difficulties. Tomorrow promises to be dark and full of despondency. You go to sleep, only to wet the pillow with tears because of unresolved issues. The morning rises with its new challenges but hardly any solutions. In this kind of situation, God is always with you. You are never alone!

Never Alone

> 'Therefore the Lord Himself will give you a sign:
> Behold, the virgin shall conceive and bear a Son,
> and shall call His name Immanuel.' Isaiah 7:14

This world is full of troubles. Sometimes the future is faced with hopelessness and dread. Everywhere you turn there is an aching heart. Children are being torn by death from their mothers' bosoms at tender ages. Every home has the suffering and the sick. Life seems to be unbearable today.

Relatives and friends tend to be at a distance when you are afflicted with trials and sufferings. Time comes when you need comfort and solace but it is not there. When your soul is full of sorrow and grief, when your life seems to be ebbing away, remember you are never alone. God is ever with you.

Yes, your friends may fail you; your relatives may not understand you; your children may fail to empathise with you, and your spouse may not give needed comfort in time of trouble, but remember, God will never fail you. He has assured his children, ' "I am with you always, to the very end of the age." ' (Matthew 28:20, NIV.) God is a Friend both in times of affliction and prosperity. Take time to smile because you are never alone!

In the Bible we read the good news about the birth of Immanuel. The Bible promises: 'Therefore the Lord himself

Never Alone

will give you a sign: The virgin will be with child and will give birth to a son, and will call him Immanuel.' (Isaiah 7:14, NIV.) That was a prophetic promise of a Saviour to the sin-sick world. Isaiah foretold the birth of Jesus long before the actual event. This means that the life of Jesus did not begin in Bethlehem. Branson reveals:

'The life of Christ did not begin in the Bethlehem manger. That was only an incarnation. He had existed from eternity. He had shared the companionship and the glory of God. Now He had voluntarily come into the world and taken upon Himself the nature of fallen man. He had been born of woman for the sole purpose of reopening the gates of Paradise to man by saving him from his sins.'[1]

A 'virgin shall conceive'. That was unique. How could a woman who had never met a man conceive? Indeed, it was not by human action but by divine intervention. God sometimes works in ways that baffle the wisdom of this world. For a virgin to conceive in the natural order of life demands her losing her virginity first. But, contrary to human reasoning, God was to provide a Saviour for humankind through a divine miracle.

Moreover, the virgin was to bear a 'son'. According to Jewish culture, a son was to be the heir of the father's heritage. Abraham and Sarah suffered mental anguish in their barrenness because there was no heir. God had promised to increase Abraham's seed, but he had no child. He wondered how God would multiply his offspring. Sons were of great value in the eyes of the Hebrew. Mary was honoured in that she was going to have a son.

According to Matthew 1:23, Jesus Christ, who is referred to as *Immanuel*, which means *'God with us'*, was to be born. At the time of Jesus' birth, the Jewish nation was under bondage to the Romans. Following the prophecy of a Deliverer, the whole Jewish race longed for a time when the 'Son' was to be born in order to deliver them from Roman bondage. Hawthorne states: 'And the birth of the young woman's son at that time was to be a sign to Judah that

Never Alone

God was with his people and with the royal line of David to deliver them from their enemy.'[2] Religious rites of the Jews were not meeting the needs of the people at the time Jesus was about to be born. They had become formal. This was one of the reasons why the Jews were looking forward to a Deliverer.

Jesus' designation as Immanuel, 'God with us', is a symbol that God will always be with his children. The 'Son of Man' was Jesus' own favourite title for himself, to emphasise his connection with humanity. Never will he leave them to suffer without any hope. God is with us. In Jesus we have a Saviour who sympathises with us. The apostle John reveals: 'And the Word became flesh and dwelt among us, and we beheld His glory, the glory as of the only begotten of the Father, full of grace and truth.'[3] Jesus Christ was born among men. He ate with men, he walked with men, and slept among men as an example of his interest in their welfare. Jesus Christ is not a 'remote-controller' being who lives at a distance while controlling the affairs of this universe. In the Exodus experience, God told the Israelites, ' "And let them make Me a sanctuary, that I may dwell among them." '[4] In instructing the children of Israel to build him a sanctuary, God was declaring his interest in being with his people. Ellen White explains:

'So Christ set up His tabernacle in the midst of our human encampment. He pitched His tent by the side of the tents of men, that He might dwell among us, and make us familiar with His divine character and life . . . Since Jesus came to dwell with us, we know that God is acquainted with our trials, and sympathizes with our griefs. Every son and daughter of Adam may understand that our Creator is the friend of sinners.'[5]

The sanctuary symbolised the presence of God. Indeed, in the construction of the temple, God was associating himself with the spiritual and physical needs of the people. In like manner, he is with and among us today. He is here as our Redeemer from physical, social, economic and spiritual dilemmas. Therefore, cheer up; you are never alone. In the

Never Alone

Scriptures God assures his children of his constant care, saying: 'But Zion said, "The Lord has forsaken me, And my Lord has forgotten me." "Can a woman forget her nursing child, And not have compassion on the son of her womb? Surely they may forget, Yet I will not forget you. See, I have inscribed you on the palms of My hands." '[6] The birth, life and death of Jesus Christ grant hope to all downtrodden souls. When we look at the birth of Jesus, we see a Redeemer. When we look at his life, we see our Example and Friend. As we look at him on the cross, we see the Lamb. When he ascends to heaven, we see the High Priest; and when we see him come in the clouds of heaven, we see a Deliverer. God is with his people at all times and seasons.

[1] William Henry Branson, *Drama of Ages* (Southern Publishing Association), pp. 58,59.
[2] Gerald F. Hawthorne, *The Presence and the Power* (Word Publishing), p. 72.
[3] John 1:14, *New King James Version*.
[4] *Ibid*. Exodus 25:8.
[5] Ellen G. White, *Desire of Ages* (Pacific Press Publishing Association), pp. 23, 24.
[6] Isaiah 49:14-16.

Never Alone

WORDS OF HOPE

Words from Scripture

'Though you have made me see troubles, many and bitter, you will restore my life again; from the depths of the earth you will again bring me up.'
Psalm 71:20.

'May the God of hope fill you with all joy and peace as you trust in him, so that you may overflow with hope by the power of the Holy Spirit.'
Romans 15:13.

'I pray also that the eyes of your heart may be enlightened in order that you may know the hope to which he has called you, the riches of his glorious inheritance in the saints, and his incomparably great power for us who believe.'
Ephesians 1:18, 19.

'Praise be to the God and Father of our Lord Jesus Christ! In his great mercy he has given us new birth into a living hope through the resurrection of Jesus Christ from the dead. . . .'
1 Peter 1:3.

' "Do not let your hearts be troubled. Trust in God; trust also in me. In my Father's house are many rooms; if it were not so, I would have told you. I am going there to prepare a place for you. And if I go and prepare a place for you, I will come back and take you to be with me that you also may be where I am." '
John 14:1-3.

Never Alone

Words from the wise

'Other men see only a hopeless end, but the Christian rejoices in an endless hope.'
Gilbert Brenken.

'What oxygen is to the lungs, such is hope for the meaning of life.'
Emil Brunner.

'The word which God has written on the brow of every man is Hope.'
Victor Hugo.

'Hope is the struggle of the soul, breaking loose from what is perishable, and attesting her eternity.'
Herman Melville.

'The future is as bright as the promises of God.'
Adoniram Judson.

'We must accept finite disappointment, but we must never lose infinite hope.'
Martin Luther King.

'The Christian message is that there is hope for a ruined humanity – hope of pardon, hope of peace with God, hope of glory – because at the Father's will Jesus Christ became poor, and was born in a stable so that thirty years later he might hang on a cross.'
J. I. Packer.

Never Alone

Chastened, but not Forsaken

> 'And they heard the sound of the Lord God walking in the garden in the cool of the day, and Adam and his wife hid themselves from the presence of the Lord God among the trees of the garden. Then the Lord God called to Adam and said to him, "Where are you?" ' Genesis 3:8, 9.

God will never forsake us, his own children. It is only disobedience that brings a barrier between God and us. Even when we go astray from God, he does not forsake us. When we miss the mark, he extends his hand for reconciliation. God created Adam and Eve for his glory and pleasure and he placed them in the Garden of Eden. He had extended his fellowship to them. Unfortunately, the pair sinned against God, and thus fear and guilt struck them. They had defied the word of God and, therefore, cut themselves off from the source of life. They were naked (Genesis 3:7) because God's glory which had been their covering departed from them. Adam and Eve forfeited life just as God's word states. Whenever man sins against God, he loses his peace of mind. No one with a sensitive conscience can live a life of happiness and joy in sin. A life devoid of the blessings of God is not satisfying. No matter what material possessions one may have in this world, that peace which satisfies the inner being comes only from God. Adam and Eve were caught in a rut of disobedience. Upon

Never Alone

hearing God's approach they hid from their Creator. In the cool of the day and with full knowledge of their disobedience, God reached out to seek the disobedient pair. In a bid to hide their nakedness, they sewed fig leaves that did not help them at all. Hiding under the foliage of Eden did not give them refuge. Moreover, can man hide from the presence of the Lord? David exclaimed:

'Where can I go from Your Spirit? Or where can I flee from your presence? If I ascend into heaven, You are there; If I make my bed in hell, behold, you are there. If I take the wings of the morning, And dwell in the uttermost parts of the sea, Even there Your hand shall lead me, And Your right hand shall hold me. If I say, "Surely the darkness shall fall on me," Even the night shall be light about me; Indeed, the darkness shall not hide from You, But the night shines as the day; The darkness and the light are both alike to You.'[1]

When God asked where Adam and Eve were, the question did not suggest that he did not know the whereabouts of the pair. God was trying to make them accountable for what they had done by giving them an opportunity to confess their disobedience. More than that, God had come down to redeem the pair. When Adam and Eve sinned, God took the initiative to save them. He came to them to confront them with their iniquity and to redeem them. Just as a shepherd seeks a lost sheep, so this is how God comes to us when we are lost from his presence. From the fall of Adam and Eve, we see God stooping low to be reconciled with the couple. This demonstrates that God will not leave his created beings to agonise in sin and afflictions. God does not condone sin, but he sympathises with those who cut themselves off from his presence because of their sin, and he goes out of his way to bring them to himself. They forfeited the beautiful home that God had originally intended them to live in. They were sent outside the garden, but were not forsaken. God continued to take care of them, by giving them another vocation, of tilling the ground (Genesis 3:23) for their sustenance, under his divine love

Never Alone

and care.

God's question to Adam and Eve, 'Where are you?' still echoes in our individual lives today. God does not want you to bear the pressures of this world alone. He is asking you to put your burdens in his hands. So he asks you, 'Where are you?' Where are you in terms of relationship with him? Where are you in relation to your response to his offer of eternal life? Where are you when faced with the difficulties of life? 'Why not come to me and let me assist you through it all?' God asks.

'When life seems tough, you are never alone!
When your choices make you fall,
There is a hand stretched out to you,
You are never alone.

When your efforts fail to satisfy your needs and desires,
Look up! You are never alone.
When the fig leaves dry up in the sun,
Simply turn to God.
When you hear Him ask, "Where are you?"
Simply respond, "Here am I; take me and give me a second chance." '

God's interest in you is immeasurable, as though you were the only creature on Earth.

You are never alone!

---

[1] Psalms 139:7-12.

WORDS OF COURAGE

Never Alone
Words from Scripture

'Do not fear, for I am with you; do not be dismayed for I am your God. I will strengthen you and help you; I will uphold you with my righteous right hand. All who rage against you will surely be ashamed and disgraced; . . . though you search for your enemies, you will not find them.' Isaiah 41:10-12.

'The Lord is a refuge for the oppressed, a stronghold in times of trouble. Those who know your name will trust in you, for you, Lord, have never forsaken those who seek you.' Psalm 9:9, 10.

'If God is for us, who can be against us? He who did not spare his own Son, but gave him up for us all – how will he not also, along with him, graciously give us all things?' Romans 8:31, 32.

' "My grace is sufficient for you, for my power is made perfect in weakness." ' 2 Corinthians 12:9.

'Do not be afraid or discouraged, for the Lord is the one who goes before you. He will be with you; he will neither fail you nor forsake you.' Deuteronomy 31:8, NLT.

'Jesus said, "Come to me, all of you who are weary and carry heavy burdens, and I will give you rest." ' Matthew 11:28, NLT.

Never Alone

Words from the wise

'Does God seem far away from you? One of you moved. And it wasn't him.'

'When the picture looks bleak don't ask God to take you out of it but to join you in it. That way everything is transformed, including you.'

'Fight fear with trust and, because God gives power upon request, joy is around the corner.'

'When you are at your weakest and most impotent is when God is best able to make you a person of power.'

'When you are buffeted by the storms of life and your decks are awash, a change of Captain may be called for.'

'When you have problems remember the Bible's words: "It came to pass" – *not to stay*. Hang in there! A new day is dawning.'

Extracts from *God's Little Book of Encouragement*.

Never Alone

The **Lord** was with **Joseph**

'The Lord was with Joseph, and he was a successful man;. . . And his master saw that the Lord was with him and that the Lord made all he did to prosper in his hand . . . and the blessing of the Lord was on all that he had in the house and in the field.'
'But the Lord was with Joseph and showed him mercy, and He gave him favour in the sight of the keeper of the prison.'
Genesis 39: 2, 3, 5, 21.

Life can be bitter if one of your closest brothers or sisters betrays you. It is a terrible experience when those you expect to help you turn against you. It is painful to endure the betrayal of your own kinsmen. Jacob had twelve sons and one daughter. Joseph's brothers, full of jealousy over his dreams and because he was their father's favourite, decided to kill him by throwing him into a pit (Genesis 37:24). After their evil deed they sat down to eat a meal (Genesis 37:25). That was how indifferent the brothers of Joseph had become. Hatred drives many friends, families, tribes and nationalities asunder. Hatred breeds death. Joseph was in a pit while the brothers sat down to eat bread. He agonised for his life while the brothers were devising ways of cheating their father in regard to his fate. Many people rejoice today when someone they hate falls into trouble. It is even more painful when fellow Christians celebrate the downfall of another brother or sister. Animals

Never Alone

often seem to be more sympathetic than human beings. Animals like cattle will surround an injured fellow creature and bellow. A dove normally lays two eggs and these hatch into male and female doves. When the two doves grow, they live together as mates. If one of them is killed, the other lives a miserable life. It has also been observed that if a male dove is killed, the female dove will seek another male that is lacking a partner. Doves enjoy a warm relationship between themselves. How one wishes human beings could emulate the love manifested by some of the creatures God has created!

In an attempt to save the brothers from shedding innocent blood, Judah suggested that Joseph be sold as a slave to the Ishmaelite traders (Genesis 37:26-28). Being a slave was worse than death, particularly when one has been sold by one's own kinsmen. Their own brother was sold as a slave to foreigners. In Egypt, Joseph again was sold to Potiphar, an officer of Pharaoh, captain of the guard (Genesis 39:1). While in Potiphar's home, Joseph was accused of attempting to rape Mrs Potiphar. The accuser was the tempter herself. Immediately, Joseph shifted residence from the captain's home to the prison.

This world is full of accusation and mockery. Sometimes innocent men and women suffer for their integrity while the guilty go free. Does God forget his children when they go through the pain of injustice? The answer is 'no'. The Bible reveals this concerning Joseph: 'The Lord was with Joseph, and he was a successful man; . . . And his master saw that the Lord was with him and that the Lord made all he did to prosper in his hand . . . and the blessing of the Lord was on all that he had in the house and in the field. . . . But the Lord was with Joseph and showed him mercy, and He gave him favour in the sight of the keeper of the prison.'
(Genesis 39: 2, 3, 5, 21.) Joseph was handled like a commodity, being handed by his brothers to the Midianites, by them to Potiphar, by Potiphar to the prison guard.

Even in prison God's hand was not limited to reach out to

Never Alone

save and to bless. Joseph's accuser landed him in prison. The innocent had his home in the prison while the guilty woman lived in luxury.

The Christian life is not a smooth road at all times. Forces of evil are at work through human beings to bring about frustration and defeat to God's children. God's children may sometimes suffer for their faith; nonetheless, God will never leave them alone. He keeps his eye upon them wherever they are.

However, God may not immediately deliver them from certain circumstances in order to vindicate his name and power. As Christians, when trials come our way, let us not despair, for God is with us. When Habakkuk cried out for God's justice against the Chaldeans who were about to attack his children, the answer was, 'But the Lord is in His holy temple. Let all the earth keep silence before Him.'[1]

God is not dethroned; he is in his holy temple. God is in the control room of this universe. Circumstances can never discourage him. He is waiting for a day when he will step out and bring justice to the land. Complaining will not help you; simply keep your silence because God is in the control room. To be silent is to trust that God is with you, that God understands your situation and that he will deliver.

God's presence was with Joseph and he brought him out of prison. Because God was with Joseph, he was able, through divine foresight, to save Egypt from the impending famine. Not only that; Joseph's entire family was saved from famine and he was made the Prime Minister of Egypt. God is leading your life, too, with keen interest. God has a plan for each person on earth so long as he/she abides in him. Though perilous times may come, God will not forsake his children.

The ravaging famine affected Joseph's family and finally they came to live in Egypt (Genesis 45-47). Reconciliation was effected. Joseph did not take revenge on his brothers for their mistreatment. To their amazement he said to them, 'But now, do not therefore be grieved or angry with

Never Alone

yourselves because you sold me here; for God sent me before you to preserve life.'[2]

God will not reach out to bless a person who rejoices in revenge. Vengeance is for the Lord to administer. The Bible admonishes: 'Beloved, do not avenge yourselves, but rather give place to wrath; for it is written, "Vengeance is mine; I will repay," says the Lord. Therefore "If your enemy is hungry, feed him; If he is thirsty, give him a drink; For in so doing you will heap coals of fire on his head." '[3] Some people feel happy when they are compensated for their mistreatment, but Joseph simply offered praise to God for preserving his life. The spirit of revenge among believers in God has brought shame to God, who has actually rescued us from worse and almost fatal situations. How can brothers and sisters of the same faith seek lawsuits, using the help of those who do not know God, as a way of arbitration? We are to live peaceably with all people.

God will never leave his children to suffer alone. The Bible declares: 'Behold, the Lord's hand is not shortened, That it cannot save; Nor His ear heavy, That it cannot hear, But your iniquities have separated you from your God; And your sins have hidden His face from you, So that He will not hear.'[4] My brothers and sisters, sometimes your closest friends can bring discouragement to you. Remember how Joseph suffered at the hands of his brothers, and yet God did not forsake him. In your case, too, in moments of gloom and shadow, remember that God will be with you always.

[1] Habakkuk 2:20.
[2] Genesis 45:5.
[3] Romans 12:19, 20.
[4] Isaiah 59:1, 2.

WORDS OF FAITH — Never Alone

Words from Scripture

'For it is by grace you have been saved, through faith – and this not from yourselves, it is the gift of God.' Ephesians 2:8.

'... If you have faith as small as a mustard seed, you can say to this mountain, "Move from here to there" and it will move. Nothing will be impossible for you.' Matthew 17:21.

'Be faithful, even to the point of death.' Revelation 2:10.

'The only thing that counts is faith expressing itself through love.' Galatians 5:6.

'Faith comes from hearing the message, and the message is heard through the word of Christ.' Romans 10:17.

'For everyone born of God overcomes the world. This is the victory that has overcome the world, even our faith.' 1 John 5:4.

Never Alone

Words from the wise

'The life of faith is continually renewed victory over doubt, a continually renewed grasp of meaning in the midst of meaninglessness.' L. Newbigin.

'A little faith will bring your soul to heaven, but a lot of faith will bring heaven to your soul.' Dwight L. Moody.

'The only saving faith is that which casts itself on God for life or death.' Martin Luther.

'Faith given back to us after a night of doubt is a stronger thing, and far more valuable to us than faith that has never been tested.' Elizabeth Goudge.

'Expect great things from God, attempt great things for God.' William Carey.

'Fear imprisons, faith liberates; fear paralyses, faith empowers; fear disheartens, faith encourages; fear sickens, faith heals; fear makes useless; faith makes serviceable; most of all, fear puts hopelessness at the heart of life; while faith rejoices in its God.' H. E. Fosdick.

'Feed your faith and starve your doubts to death!' Andrew Murray.

Never Alone

Under the **Pillars** of **Cloud** and **Fire**

'And the Lord went before them by day in a pillar of cloud to lead the way, and by night in a pillar of fire to give them light, so as to go by day and night. He did not take away the pillar of cloud by day or the pillar of fire by night from before the people.'
Exodus 13:21, 22.

They had been in Egypt for too long and the time had come when Israel had to be led out of the land of bondage. They needed to go back to Canaan so that God could fulfil his plans for them. They had served the Egyptians for four hundred years but then the time had come to go and serve the God of Israel. They were to go and take back their heritage. Israel at that juncture had no trained army to protect them on their journey to Canaan. They were not militarily prepared for any war should their enemies attack them. For that reason, God manifested himself in a pillar of cloud by day and fire by night. The Bible says, 'And the Lord went before them. . . .' God did not want his children to go to Canaan unprotected. He decided to go with them. It is good to know that in moments of your helplessness, God is willing to lead the way for you. Dybdahl points out:

'God does not just bring Israel out of Egypt and then leave her to fend for herself. He gives a constant reminder and evidence of His presence. The daytime reminder is a pillar of cloud, and the nighttime is a pillar of fire. One or the other is always present.

Never Alone

The stated purpose of these twin "pillars" is to guide the people and give them light. They can thus know where to go and at night have light to go where guided. Underlying all this, of course, is the surety that God is there, and where they are going is where He wants them to be.'[1]

God will not bid us do something for which he himself has not provided resources. God went before them and he was with them throughout the journey. He did not abandon them at any point. God will never forsake his children. Things may appear confused but God leads his people.

During the wilderness journey, God appeared to the children of Israel during the day in the form of the pillar of cloud. The cloud was to give them shade from the hot desert sun. The cloud was visible during the day. When it moved forward, Israel moved forward as well. When the cloud stopped moving, Israel, too, stood still, awaiting further marching orders. God likewise is interested in guiding us during our day-to-day activities. He is willing to lead us in safe paths. He is a sheltering cloud for our hearts today. The question is, 'Are you in the hands of God so that he can lead you in the way you should go?' It is a dangerous thing to move ahead of God, for in so doing you remove yourself from his protecting presence. Every morning ask God to show you what to do. Do not move in this world without God's protection. Ask him to show you the way to tread each day. You only know what yesterday was, but not what today and tomorrow will be. It is safe to seek God's guidance in all that we do.

God was 'by night . . . a pillar of fire to give them light'. In the wilderness it was cold at night, therefore the pillar of fire provided warmth to them and light for the way. God wanted to protect Israel at night. Under the shadow of night many evil things take place. It is at night that a thief usually breaks in to steal, and it is at night that an enemy strikes. At night the way was not clear, but God decided to be a way to Israel. God keeps watch over us at night; he does not slumber; he is a faithful watchman. We need God's

Never Alone

protection at all times. At no time can man live without God. At the same time, our Christian journey should not be static. By night and by day, we must be spiritually awake. The Exodus was to continue by day and by night; so must our spiritual exodus from sin keep moving. As long as Israel remained faithful to God, the way was safe to the Promised Land. Ellen White declares:

'Christ was the leader of the children of Israel in their wilderness wanderings. Enshrouded in the pillar of cloud by day and the pillar of fire by night, He led and guided them. He preserved them from the perils of the wilderness, He brought them into the land of promise, and in the sight of all the nations that acknowledged not God He established Israel as His own chosen possession, the Lord's vineyard.'[2]

Most of the Israelites detached themselves from the source of life and did not reach the Promised Land. Of that generation, all died in the wilderness except Caleb and Joshua. In the case of those who remained loyal to God, regardless of the snares on the journey, God guided them to the Promised Land. They crossed the Red Sea on dry ground. God will surely be with us all the time. He promised, ' "and lo, I am with you always, even to the end of the age" ',[3] and God is not man that he can lie. He is with us today. The Holy Spirit is here to guide us into all truth. He is our Comforter and he sympathises with all our cares. Regardless of many snares that beset us, God is with us. We are never alone!

[1] Jon L. Dybdahl, *The Abundant Life Bible Amplifier: Exodus* (Pacific Press Publishing Association), p. 129.
[2] Ellen G. White, *Christ's Object Lessons* (Review and Herald Publishing Association), p 287.
[3] Matthew 28:20

Never Alone

WORDS OF GRACE

Words from Scripture

'Are you tired? Worn out? Burned out on religion? Come to me. Get away with me and you'll recover your life. I'll show you how to take a real rest. Walk with me and work with me – watch how I do it. Learn the unforced rhythms of grace.' Jesus, in Matthew 11:28-30 (Message paraphrase).

'Now God has us where he wants us, with all the time in this world and the next to shower grace and kindness upon us in Christ Jesus. Saving is all his idea, and all his work. All we do is trust him enough to let him do it.' Ephesians 2:7-9 (Message paraphrase).

'I am convinced that neither death nor life, . . . neither angels nor demons, neither the present nor the future, nor any powers, neither height nor depth, nor anything else in all creation, will be able to separate us from the love of God that is in Christ Jesus our Lord.' Romans 8:38, 39.

'God . . . is our Father and the source of all mercy and comfort. For he gives us comfort in all our trials so that we in turn may be able to give the same sort of strong sympathy to others in their troubles that we receive from God.' 2 Corinthians 1:3-5, (Phillips paraphrase).

' "Hey there! All who are thirsty, come to the water! Are you penniless? Come anyway – buy and eat! . . . Buy without money – everything's free." ' Isaiah 55:1 (Message paraphrase).

Never Alone

Words from the wise

'Grace is the free, undeserved goodness and favour of God to mankind.' Matthew Henry.

'I am not what I ought to be; I am not what I wish to be; I am not what I hope to be; but by the grace of God I am what I am.' John Newton.

'Cheap grace is grace without discipleship, grace without the cross, grace without Jesus Christ, living and incarnate.' Dietrich Bonhoeffer.

'It is grace at the beginning, and grace at the end. So that when you and I come to lie upon our deathbeds the one thing that should comfort and help and strengthen us there is the thing that helped us in the beginning. Not what we have been, not what we have done, but the grace of God in Jesus Christ our Lord. The Christian life starts with grace, it must continue with grace, it ends with grace. God's wondrous grace. By the grace of God I am what I am, yet not I, but the grace of God which was with me.' D. Martyn Lloyd-Jones.

'Grace is not simply leniency when we have sinned. Grace is the enabling gift of God not to sin. Grace is power, not just pardon.' John Piper.

'Your worst days are never so bad that you are beyond the reach of God's grace. And your best days are never so good that you are beyond the need of God's grace.' Jerry Bridges.

Never Alone

Forty Years Feeding on One Dish

'And the children of Israel ate manna forty years, until they came to an inhabited land; they ate manna until they came to the border of the land of Canaan.' Exodus 16:35.

On the journey from Egypt to the Promised Land, the children of Israel were fed on manna for forty years. That was the best diet for them. They fed on one type of food and never suffered from malnutrition, an indication that food which comes from the hand of the Maker is always nutritious. In providing manna for Israel, God was demonstrating his interest in the physical well-being of his people. God created us and so he knows that which is best for man. By providing manna, God also demonstrated his ability to provide for his creation. Jesus Christ is the bread of life (John 6:35, 48). Just as God provided manna for Israel, he is also able to provide for our physical needs today. In a journey lasting forty years, God was able to provide for the daily needs of his people. For forty years, he proved his ability to do so. God's resources are indeed bountiful. Our Lord drew a comparison between himself and the manna sent down from heaven (John 6:41).

Hunger is an enemy to man. Moreover, hungry people are hard to manage. Strikes hit companies because of a desire to meet physical needs. Hunger sometimes compels people to steal or work on the Sabbath day, thus violating God's

Never Alone

Law. Some women become sex workers because of trying to meet physical needs. Some parents allow their daughters to marry at an early age in order to earn a living. Some people go to the extent of selling their own children. Parents disown their own children on account of the biting economy. Some women have abortions for fear of failing to get means to look after their babies. In the miracle of manna given to the children of Israel, God was showing us that he is able to provide for our physical needs in every circumstance. But it was the responsibility of the Israelites to go out and gather the manna, which demonstrates that man must co-operate with God in order to get that which benefits him. The Bible says: 'Six days you shall labour and do all your work.'[1] God does not delight in indolence. We must work to earn our own bread. When man co-operates with God, miracles *do* happen and man's physical needs are met.

Do not worry about providing meals for tomorrow. Your principal concern should be, 'Am I in the hands of God? Is God my Shepherd and am I a loyal sheep?' What a comfort to know that there is nothing to fear for our physical needs because we are not alone; God is the Master Provider who is interested in our well-being.

[1] Exodus 20:9.

Never Alone

WORDS OF LOVE

Words from Scripture

'Many waters cannot quench love; rivers cannot wash it away.' Song of Solomon 8:7.

'And over all these virtues put on love, which binds them all together in perfect unity.' Colossians 3:14.

'May the Lord make your love increase and overflow for each other and for everyone else, just as ours does for you.' 1 Thessalonians 3:12.

'For God so loved the world that he gave his one and only Son, that whoever believes in him shall not perish but have eternal life.' Jesus in John 3:16.

'But God demonstrates his own love for us in this: While we were still sinners Christ died for us.' Romans 5:8.

Never Alone
Words from the wise

'Christianity does not think of a man finally submitting to the power of God, it thinks of him as finally surrendering to the love of God. It is not that man's will is crushed, but that man's heart is broken.'
William Barclay.

'Increase my capacity for love and decrease my impulses to throw stones, actual or mental.'
George Appleton.

'For the love of God is broader
Than the measures of man's mind;
And the heart of the Eternal
Is most wonderfully kind.'
F. W. Faber.

'Love is the sum of all virtue, and love disposes us to do good.'
Jonathan Edwards.

Never Alone

Water from the Rock in the Desert

' "Behold, I will stand before you there on the rock in Horeb; and you shall strike the rock, and water will come out of it, that the people may drink." And Moses did so in the sight of the elders of Israel.' Exodus 17:6.

The children of Israel were then in the wilderness. It was dry, no water was available and the people were thirsty, so they complained bitterly against Moses and against God. The livestock of the Israelites were about to perish. But while the people complained, God had already provided for them. God had trapped water for them in a rock. He is not controlled by circumstances but has the ability to provide for all of our needs, even from unexpected places. If we trust in God, he will do that which we are unable to do for ourselves. Water is assured to those who seek God earnestly. Jesus is the spring of the Living Water (John 4:10). No one who comes to him will be thirsty. Those who ate manna and drank the water in the wilderness *did* hunger and thirst for water again, but those who come to the Lord will lack nothing; these are sure words of promise.

It must be clearly understood that God is the One who provides for our needs. He has the ability to give us food, clothing, children, education and health. Let us tell our Father who has unnumbered resources and then we have nothing to fear for our physical needs. Economies of this

Never Alone

world do collapse, yet God's ability to provide for human beings is unlimited. He alone cannot be given economic sanctions. His bank can never be liquidated. You cannot have an overdraft in God's account. Companies get liquidated and become defunct, but God's ability to provide can never be exhausted. You can learn to put your trust in God who has power to do all things for you. God is able to provide manna in the desert, even where it is impossible to grow anything. From a rock God provided water. Leaving the poverty of this world, you can be a millionaire when you co-operate with God in your plans. You can rise from nothing to something. There is treasure in the storehouse of God.

Never Alone

WORDS OF SALVATION

Words from Scripture

'Salvation is found in no-one else [than Jesus Christ], for there is no other name under heaven given to men by which we must be saved.' Acts 4:12.

'Therefore, my dear friends, as you have always obeyed – not only in my presence, but now much more in my absence – continue to work out your salvation with fear and trembling, for it is God who works in you to will and to act according to his good purpose.' Philippians 2:12, 13.

'He was pierced for our transgressions, he was crushed for our iniquities; the punishment that brought us peace was upon him, and by his wounds we are healed.' Isaiah 53:5.

'For Christ died for sins once for all, the righteous for the unrighteous, to bring you to God. He was put to death in the body but made alive by the Spirit.' 1 Peter 3:18.

'For it is by grace you have been saved, through faith – and this not from yourselves, it is the gift of God – not by works, so that no one can boast. For we are God's workmanship.' Ephesians 2:8-10.

'But now in Christ Jesus you who once were far away have been brought near through the blood of Christ.' Ephesians 2:13.

'May I never boast except in the cross of our Lord Jesus Christ, through which the world has been crucified to me, and I to the world.' Galatians 6:14.

Never Alone

Words from the wise

'We must first be made good before we can do good; we must first be made just before our works can please God.' Hugh Latimer.

'There is no more urgent and critical question in life than that of your personal relationship with God and your eternal salvation.' Billy Graham.

'The fundamental principles of Christianity are these two: the doctrine of justification, and that of the new birth; the former relating to that great work God does for us, in forgiving our sins; the latter to the great work of God in us, in renewing our fallen nature.' John Wesley.

'Christians are not men and women who are hoping for salvation, but those who have experienced it.' D. Martyn Lloyd-Jones.

'If man could have saved himself there would have been no need for the Son of God to come on earth. Indeed, his coming is proof that people cannot save themselves.' D. Martyn Lloyd-Jones.

Never Alone

Four out of Three

'Then king Nebuchadnezzar was astonished; and he rose in haste and spoke, saying to his counsellors, "Did we not cast three men bound into the midst of the fire?" They answered and said to the king, "True, O king." "Look!" he answered, "I see four men loose, walking in the midst of the fire; and they are not hurt, and the form of the fourth is like the Son of God." ' Daniel 3:24, 25.

Nebuchadnezzar, King of Babylon, had set up an image in the plain of Dura (Daniel 3:1-30). It was required that every inhabitant of Babylon worship that image in honour of King Nebuchadnezzar. According to the Jews, the worshipping of idols was an act of disobedience to the Creator of heaven and earth. The three Hebrew youths who were taken captive to Babylon became the centre of attention concerning that decree. Shadrach, Meshach and Abednego, servants of the Most High God, knew from their childhood that worshipping images was a sign of disobedience. They knew that only God was worthy of worship. Only God, who transcends all kings and princes, should receive adoration. The decree posed a challenge and it was in the power of the three Hebrew youths to honour God or to dishonour him. It was within their power to rationalise the truth and simply comply with the decree from the King. These young men under the threat of death could have found an excuse to worship the image momentarily and after that revert to worshipping God.

Never Alone

But, on the contrary, the young men decided not to please Nebuchadnezzar but rather to please God. Uriah Smith says:

'Their answer was both honest and decisive. "We are not careful," said they, "to answer thee in this matter." That is, you need not grant us the favour of another trial; our minds are made up. We can answer as well now as at any future time; and our answer is, We will not serve thy gods, nor worship the golden image which thou hast set up. Our God can deliver if He so desires; but if not, we shall not complain. We know His will, and we shall render Him unconditional obedience.'[1]

Their decision to stand for God was a decision to be thrown into the fiery furnace. The furnace was heated seven times hotter than usual which implies that it was extremely hot. Regardless of the fiery furnace, the Hebrew youths made a choice to stand for that which was right. All of us at times are brought into situations that require us to choose between right and wrong. Those who love their God will always stand for the right, regardless of the consequences. Their focus will be on God and not on the consequences. If you give the devil an inch of loyalty, then he will demand a mile of your life in disobedience.

Once upon a time, a university graduate suffered when looking for a job on account of Sabbath-keeping. This young man had sought employment, and due to his good qualifications he had many job offers, but on account of keeping the Sabbath of the Lord as revealed in the Scriptures (Exodus 20:8-11; Ezekiel 20:20), he could not take up the offers. He remained unemployed for some years. Finally he was offered a job with many other benefits. The interviewer asked him whether he would be willing to work during the Sabbath hours, Friday sunset to Saturday sunset. The young man looked back and pondered on how he had suffered unemployment, because of his Sabbath-keeping. Finally, he resolved the issue and replied, 'Yes, I will work once in a while if there is work on Sabbath.' Then the prospective employer said, 'If you cannot be faithful to your

Never Alone

God, as I know you to be a Sabbath-keeper, then how can you be faithful to this company?' Let us be willing to be faithful to God, even if it requires us to be poor or jobless.

One case of unfaithfulness, although only temporary, will not bring us any blessings from God. One inch of self-pleasing in indulging in sin will invite death as a reward. The decision to eat a fruit in the Garden of Eden brought about death and decay. Simple as the act seemed, it was a demonstration of loyalty to the deceiver and so a choice of death. Sin cannot be justified, no matter what situation one is in, because God has provided a way of escape out of every temptation we face. The Bible says: 'No temptation has overtaken you except such as is common to man; but God is faithful, who will not allow you to be tempted beyond what you are able, but with the temptation will also make the way of escape, that you may be able to bear it.'[2] To give any excuse for sin is to regard Jesus Christ's death on Calvary as in vain.

The Hebrew boys refused to bow to the threats of the King, resulting in their being thrown into the fiery furnace. God has promised never to leave us alone. The question in the minds of the Hebrew boys was: 'Will our God save us?' Will God fail his own servants who are standing for the truth? Where are the angels at this moment? What is the situation like in the courts of heaven? To the onlooker, that was the end of the three boys. Everyone returned home thinking those who had defied the King's decree were no more.

When King Nebuchadnezzar went to look in the furnace to reassure himself of his power, he was astonished to see people walking in the midst of fire. 'How can this be?' could be the question of the King. The three Hebrew youths were spared from the harm of the fire. What a miracle! Moreover, there were *four* people. They threw into the furnace three people, but the King saw four people. God shielded the Hebrew youths from the burning fire. Those who fight God's faithful servants actually fight God himself. You cannot fight God and win. Sometimes evil forces may seem to triumph,

Never Alone

but God will always win. There is nothing to fear if we take God at his word. God will never leave his children alone. Nebuchadnezzar was confused, and in desperation asked the question, ' "Did we not cast three men bound into the midst of the fire?" ' (Daniel 3:24.) Three were thrown into the fire, but four appeared in the furnace. The fourth man's appearance was described by Nebuchadnezzar as being like the 'Son of God'.

Jesus Christ had come down to save his children. If God has a special appointment for you, no matter what the threats to your life may be, he will uphold your life. Three were thrown into the fire but four people appeared and the fourth was 'like the Son of God' (Daniel 3:25). God will never leave his children to suffer affliction alone. When you go through suffering of any kind, do not despair. God is there with you. When life does not seem to go right with you to the extent of your feeling suicidal, remember, God is there to redeem you.

The story of Jesus Christ coming down from heaven to be with his servants in the fire is an indication that God has a special interest in all his children. Though this world may burn around us like a fiery furnace, God's protection of his children is sure. God is Immanuel, 'God with us'. He will never leave you alone. Never alone! What a comforting thought! Friendships may break; children may go their own way; your employers may frustrate you; know that you are not alone. Like the three Hebrew boys, never think there are only the 'three' of you; you are 'four', and the fourth is the King of the Universe.

In the story of the fiery furnace, we see God at work in delivering his children. Anderson reveals:

'These are more than children's stories. They are revelations of God's power to deliver His servants who put their trust in Him. The central figure in the story of the fiery furnace is neither the king nor the courageous Hebrews, but the Son of God whom the king saw walking in the fire.'[3]

Never Alone

Never alone, even in the midst of fiery trials. So stand up and be counted among the heroes and heroines of this world. Face the world with courage – for you are never alone.

[1] Uriah Smith, *Daniel and the Revelation* (Southern Publishing Association), p. 73.
[2] 1 Corinthians 10:13.
[3] Roy Allan Anderson, *Unfolding Daniel's Prophecies* (Pacific Press Publishing Association), p.62.

WORDS OF PRAYER

Never Alone

Words from Scripture

'Be . . . faithful in prayer.' Romans 12:12.

'I pray that you may have the power to comprehend, with all the saints, what is the breadth and length and height and depth, and to know the love of Christ that surpasses knowledge, so that you may be filled with all the fullness of God.' Ephesians 3:18, 19, NRSV.

'And pray in the Spirit on all occasions with all kinds of prayers and requests. With this in mind, be alert and always keep on praying for all the saints.' Ephesians 6:18.

'Devote yourselves to prayer, being watchful and thankful.' Colossians 4:2.

'The prayer of a righteous man is powerful and effective.' James 5:16.

'The Lord is near. Do not be anxious about anything, but in everything, by prayer and petition, with thanksgiving, present your requests to God. And the peace of God, which transcends all understanding, will guard your hearts and your minds in Christ Jesus.' Phillipians 4:5-7.

Never Alone

Words from the wise

'Prayer is weakness leaning on omnipotence.' W. S. Bowden.

'Prayer is not conquering God's reluctance, but taking hold of God's willingness.' Phillips Brooks.

'Pray not for crutches but for wings.' Phillips Brooks.

'God's cause is committed to men; God commits himself to men. Praying men are the vice-regents of God; they do his work and carry out his plans.' E. M. Bounds.

'I do not pray for a lighter load, but for a stronger back.' Phillips Brooks.

'Do not make prayer a monologue – make it a conversation.' Author unknown.

'If an army advances on its stomach, a church advances on its knees.' Author unknown.

'Prayer does not change God's mind, it changes ours.' Author unknown.

Never Alone

When Enemies Plot

'Now the king went to his palace and spent the night fasting; and no musicians were brought before him. Also his sleep went from him. Then the king arose very early in the morning and went in haste to the den of lions. And when he came to the den, he cried out with a lamenting voice to Daniel. The king spoke, saying to Daniel, "Daniel, servant of the living God, has your God, whom you serve continually, been able to deliver you from the lions?" Then Daniel said to the king, "O king, live forever! My God sent His angel and shut the lions' mouths, so that they have not hurt me, because I was found innocent before Him; and also, O king, I have done no wrong before you." Now the king was exceedingly glad for him, and commanded that they should take Daniel up out of the den. So Daniel was taken up out of the den, and no injury whatever was found on him, because he believed in his God. And the king gave the command, and they brought those men who had accused Daniel, and they cast them into the den of lions – them, their children, and their wives; and the lions overpowered them, and broke all their bones in pieces before they ever came to the bottom of the den.' Daniel 6:18-24.

At that time Daniel was in Babylon. It was during the reign of Darius, the King of the Medo-Persian Empire, that Daniel was appointed as a governor. Among the three governors who were appointed, Daniel was the highest-ranking officer (Daniel 6:1-3) among the Jews in a foreign land. This key

Never Alone

position incited jealousy among his colleagues. Because of this, his workmates conspired to find a charge against him that would lead to his downfall.

Many people in blind jealousy have sought to remove others from their due and rightful positions. How do you react when your superior is less educated and qualified for the job than you? Do you have the patience to wait for the time when God will put you in leadership, or do you conspire against your colleague? Daniel found himself betrayed by his co-workers. Terrible temptations sometimes come from those who are close to us. A lot of talebearing has been borne by those we confide in. Mortal man can be deceitful. The Bemba people of Zambia have a proverb that says: *'ameno mafupa'* which literally means, 'Teeth are simply bones'. Not all who smile with you are with or for you.

Daniel was an innocent man and he had done nothing evil against his friends. He was simply executing duties on behalf of the state, and yet his friends conspired against him. This is a lesson to us that we have an adversary, the devil, who is not happy with us. Many times the devil will find accusations against God's children that will tend to tarnish the name of God. Kennedy makes this observation concerning Daniel in the den of lions: 'We have a record which is of immense practical value to the persecuted servants of God in all ages, of a great deliverance wrought by God on behalf of his faithful servant Daniel.'[1] God is willing and able to deliver his children from the snares of the evil one at all times. He is omnipotent.

The decree was passed to bar Daniel from worshipping his God for thirty days (Daniel 6:5-9). Daniel had so exemplified purity of character that it was absolutely impossible to find fault with his daily life. What set Daniel apart from his fellow princes was his good relationship with God. That was to be their basis of attack. What a character to emulate in Daniel! He lived a life of exemplary conduct. What is *your* conduct like in your family and in your community? Can it be said of you: here is a faultless person

Never Alone

in our community?

Daniel was not threatened by a decree from the King. The lions never intimidated him. He maintained his loyalty to God, and continued worshipping him as his custom was. Maxwell finds: 'Even when threatened with a lions' den, Daniel prayed – and "gave thanks" – as consistently as always.'[2] Those who have anchored their lives in God will not withdraw from duty or the path of righteousness, even when there are penalties or threats of death. God is looking for such men and women today who will stand for him in this sinful world. There is a lot of injustice in this world; faithful people are pulled down while evil men tend to prosper. Yet in spite of all this, we need men who will stand for the truth at all times. Ellen White says:

'The greatest want of the world is the want of men – men who will not be bought or sold, men who in their inmost souls are true and honest, men who do not fear to call sin by its right name, men whose conscience is as true to duty as the needle to the pole, men who will stand for the right though the heavens fall.'[3]

The decree was passed and Daniel was trapped. Sometimes evil forces tend to succeed, even when we are close to God. There is no 'royal road' for Christians. Evil men seem to triumph for a while. When such happens, do not tremble, because this does not mean that God has abandoned you. Indeed, Daniel was thrown into the den of lions. Lions are carnivorous animals and just one lion's roar makes most people shudder. Daniel was thrown into the lions' den and a stone was laid on the mouth of the den (Daniel 6:17). The King was troubled because he loved Daniel, but the King had already signed the law which could not be revoked. When you are faced with a situation that you cannot change, it is better to take the matter to God. God is never taken by surprise; he steps in to save the situation. The hungry lions' appetite for blood was quenched. The den became what it will be like in the new earth, where a lion and a man will live together. The angel of the Lord came down to

Never Alone

shut the lions' mouths. God demonstrates his ability to cripple the enemy's weapons.

A story from Nkumbi in Zambia tells of two literature evangelists who were to deliver some books to a Sergeant Chipoya. He had ordered the books and at the time he was guarding Nkumbi Bridge that had once been bombed by Rhodesian soldiers during the Zimbabwean liberation war. Innocently, the two literature evangelists decided to use a path that was a shortcut to the roadblock where Sergeant Chipoya was waiting for the delivery of books. Unfortunately, the path went through a restricted area. Within a short time, a cry went out, 'We are invaded!' Apparently the restricted area was an armoury, used by soldiers guarding the Nkumbi Bridge. The two literature evangelists were arrested and tied up. The soldiers poured petrol on them and they were made to roll on the ground, ready to be burnt to ashes. The pair cried out in desperation, entreating the soldiers to release them as all they wanted was to deliver books to Sergeant Chipoya who had placed an order with them. Their plea landed on deaf ears. Other soldiers were busy looking for matchsticks to light the pair, but none had any to start a fire. At that very moment, Sergeant Chipoya arrived at the camp from other duties. Hoping to get some credit, some soldiers immediately led Sergeant Chipoya to the spot where the pair who claimed to have business with him were tied. Sergeant Chipoya drew closer to identify the pair. He asked, 'Are you Chisenga?' And the literature evangelist answered without hesitation, even answering beyond the question: 'I am Chisenga whom you told to deliver some books to you, and we simply used a footpath to reach you.' Sergeant Chipoya turned to his fellow soldiers and asked, 'Friends, didn't they tell you about me?' With that the men were freed. Doesn't this show that God is at work even today? He is ever caring for and protecting his faithful followers.

When the King asked Daniel about the secret of his experience with the lions, Daniel's reply was, 'My God sent His angel and shut the lions' mouths, so that they have not

Never Alone

hurt me, because I was found innocent before Him; and also, O King, I have done no wrong before you.' Daniel's response needs a closer look. He addressed God as, 'My God'. Is God *your* God? How is your relationship with God? Let us take God as our personal Saviour and Redeemer. Let us walk with him in times of sorrow and in times of joy. Daniel gave glory to God for his deliverance; we ought to do the same, praising God for the great things he does for us.

It is also amazing to discover that God did not send a retinue of angels to intervene in the den; only one angel was enough to defend Daniel. Heaven can never be empty or bankrupt of resources to protect God's people. Daniel was innocent of all the accusations of his colleagues. Innocence pays. Shea establishes that 'God did not desert Daniel in the lions' den just as He did not desert Daniel's three friends in the fiery furnace. As on the earlier occasion, He sent His angel to be with Daniel and to protect him.'[4]

King Darius, therefore, commanded that Daniel be brought out of the den. At the same time he ordered the accusers of Daniel to be cast into the den instead. The golden rule is fair. It states: 'And just as you want men to do to you, you also do to them likewise.'[5] God is fair in all his dealings. The Bible further discloses:

'Do not be deceived, God is not mocked; for whatever a man sows, that he will also reap. For he who sows to his flesh will of the flesh reap corruption, but he who sows to the Spirit will of the Spirit reap everlasting life. And let us not grow weary while doing good, for in due season we shall reap if we do not lose heart. Therefore, as we have opportunity, let us do good to all, especially to those who are of the household of faith.'[6]

God teaches us to forgive those who sin against us. But those who do not repent will on the Day of Judgment meet God's retribution. The same lions that failed to eat Daniel ate his accusers. A friend of mine told me a story of a married woman who wanted to kill her husband in order to marry a rich man. On this fateful day she put poison in the local sweet beer known as *mutete*. The wife immediately excused

Never Alone

herself by visiting her friend within the village. As soon as she left, her father arrived from another direction, visiting this family. The visitor was given a seat and the son-in-law gave this sweet beer to his father-in-law, who took it enthusiastically for he was very thirsty. After some minutes the poison reacted badly. The visitor began vomiting and sweating heavily while gasping for breath, and within an hour he was dead. When the wife returned, she discovered that she had killed her father instead of her husband! She wept miserably because she knew what she had done; and because her conscience troubled her she narrated the ordeal to her relatives. Among the lessons we can learn is to be careful in life lest what we do to others turns up against us! Humankind was created in the image of God. We are all equals. We are from the same stock regardless of status, colour or background. Remember that the devil can use fellow men to trap us into sin. Moreover, when we are trapped into sin, the devil rejoices. But God is ever present to rescue us from any danger we face. If we make God our defender, he will not fail us, no matter what we may face in life. God does not leave us alone, '. . . for he who touches you touches the apple of His eye.'[7] Praise God; you are never alone!

[1] John Kennedy, *The Book of Daniel From the Christian Stand Point* (Eyre and Spottiswoode), p. 82.
[2] C. Mervyn Maxwell, *God Cares Vol. 1* (Pacific Press Publishing Association), p. 101.
[3] Ellen G. White, *Education* (Pacific Press Publishing Association), p. 57.
[4] William H. Shea, *The Abundant Life Bible Amplifier. Daniel 1-7* (Pacific Press Publishing Association), p. 124.
[5] Luke 6:31.
[6] Galatians 6:7-10.
[7] Zechariah 2:8.

WORDS OF JOY — Never Alone

Words from Scripture

'Surely God is my salvation;
I will trust and not be afraid. . . .
With joy you will draw water from the wells of salvation.'
Isaiah 12:2, 3.

'Be joyful always.'
1 Thessalonians 5:16.

'Let all who take refuge in you be glad.
Let them ever sing for joy.'
Psalm 5:11.

'You have made known to me the path of life;
You will fill me with joy in your presence. . . .'
Psalm 16:11.

'The ransomed of the Lord will return.
They will enter Zion with singing;
Everlasting joy will crown their heads.
Gladness and joy will overtake them,
And sorrow and sighing will flee away.' Isaiah 35:10.

'A woman giving birth to a child has pain because her time has come; but when her baby is born she forgets the anguish because of her joy that a child is born into the world. So with you: Now is your time of grief, but I will see you again and you will rejoice, and no-one will take away your joy.' Jesus in John 16:21, 22.

'The Lord is my strength and my shield;
my heart trusts in him, and I am helped.
My heart leaps for joy
And I will give thanks to him in song.
The Lord is the strength of his people.' Psalm 28:7, 8.

Never Alone

Words from the wise

J Jesus
O Others
Y Yourself
'If you use the JOY rule and think of Jesus, then others, then yourself, you will really feel true joy.' Author unknown.

'Joy is the experience of knowing that you are unconditionally loved.' Henri Nouwen.

'Those who bring sunshine to the lives of others cannot keep it from themselves.' James M. Barrie.

'Joy is the most infallible sign of the presence of God.' Leon Bloy.

'Joy is never in our power, and pleasure is. I doubt whether anyone who has tasted joy would ever, if both were in his power, exchange it for all the pleasure in the world.' C. S. Lewis.

'Christ is not only a remedy for your weariness and trouble, but he will give you an abundance of the contrary, joy and delight.' Jonathan Edwards.

'The opposite of joy is not sorrow. It is unbelief.' Leslie Weatherhead.

'To be able to find joy in another's joy, that is the secret of happiness.' George Bernanos.

'Joy is the serious business of heaven.' C. S. Lewis.

Never Alone

In the **Valley** of **Death** – I

'But when Herod's birthday was celebrated, the daughter of Herodias danced before them and pleased Herod. Therefore he promised with an oath to give her whatever she might ask. So she, having been prompted by her mother, said, "Give me John the Baptist's head here on a platter." And the king was sorry; nevertheless, because of the oaths and because of those who sat with him, he commanded it to be given to her. So he sent and had John beheaded in prison. And his head was brought on a platter and given to the girl, and she brought it to her mother. Then his disciples came and took away the body and buried it, and went and told Jesus.' Matthew 14:6-12.

John the Baptist was an ardent believer in God. He was the forerunner of Jesus Christ. He even had the privilege of baptising Jesus Christ. Jesus speaks of John the Baptist thus: ' "Assuredly, I say to you, among those born of women there has not risen one greater than John the Baptist." '[1] Jesus recognised that John the Baptist was indeed a great man in the eyes of heaven. He stood in the wilderness preaching the truth about repentance and rebuking sin. He was simply the hero of faith at that time. He did not fear to rebuke Herod when he married his brother's wife and that rebuke ultimately led to his arrest. He was put in prison on account of his rebuking of sin. He condemned lawlessness, and suffered the consequences. This reminds us that those

Never Alone

who live a life of purity may suffer deprivation.

During Herod's birthday celebration, the daughter of Herodias danced and amused all those who were present, to the extent that King Herod, in his excitement, promised to give her anything she wanted. Unfortunately, through the influence of her mother who hated John (Matthew 14:8), Herodias's daughter asked for the head of John the Baptist to be brought on a platter. This portrays the kind of influence mothers can have on their children. It was with Rebekah, his mother, that Jacob connived to take the blessing from Esau. It was through Eve that sin came into the world. It was through Sarah that Abraham went in to Hagar the maid and bore a son – Ishmael. Mothers can exert power for good and also for evil.

John the Baptist was beheaded. Sometimes we wonder why God's faithful servants die. One could ask, 'Where was God when John the Baptist was beheaded?' But did God surely neglect him? Would such a story inspire the faithful, that God would let them lose their lives on his account without rescuing them? Well, God will not always protect us from danger. He will not all the time prevent calamities and situations that may take our lives. He may allow suffering and even death to come upon us, but all for a purpose. When calamity strikes, it does not mean that he is incapable and uncaring. He may allow such events to come in our lives in order to glorify his name and to strengthen the courage of those who know us for what we are, just ordinary people who are ready to put our trust in him. This will also be a sign that in this world there are men and women who are able and willing to stand for God, even at the risk of loss of life. Ellen White reveals concerning John the Baptist that 'Jesus did not interpose to deliver His servant. He knew that John would bear the test.'[2] The blood of the martyr would act as a seed of encouragement and emulation to the followers of Jesus Christ. Therefore, even if death should come upon us, we must not despair. God will not have forsaken us. He will be with us even in death. He will never forget any who pay

Never Alone

the ultimate price for him (Hebrews 11:37-40). A life in Christ is not always a life of ease and peace. Trials of sickness and death may come our way. John the Baptist was killed, even though he was a faithful follower of Jehovah, yet he died, knowing he would inherit the kingdom of God.

[1] Matthew 11:11.
[2] Ellen G. White, *Desire of Ages*, p. 224.

Never Alone

WORDS OF PEACE

Words from Scripture

'Peace I leave with you; my peace I give you. I do not give to you as the world gives. Do not let your hearts be troubled and do not be afraid.' Jesus in John 14:27.

'The fruit of righteousness will be peace; the effect of righteousness will be quietness and confidence for ever.' Isaiah 32:17.

'Since we have been made right in God's sight by faith, we have peace with God because of what Jesus Christ our Lord has done for us.' Romans 5:1, NLT.

'The Lord gives strength to his people;
The Lord blesses his people with peace.' Psalm 29:11.

'You will keep in perfect peace him whose mind is steadfast, because he trusts in you' Isaiah 26:3.

'Great peace have they who love your law, and nothing can make them stumble.' Psalm 119:165.

Jesus said, 'You may find your peace in me. You will find trouble in the world – but, never lose heart, I have conquered the world!' John 16:33 (Phillips paraphrase).

'The meek will inherit the land and enjoy great peace.' Psalm 37:11.

Never Alone

Words from the wise

'Peace reigns where our Lord reigns.'
Julian of Norwich.

'Peace and justice are two sides of the same coin.'
Dwight D. Eisenhower.

'Peace hath her victories. No less renowned than war.'
John Milton.

'Peace cannot be achieved through violence, it can only be attained through understanding.'
Ralph Waldo Emmerson.

'When Christ came into the world, peace was sung; and when he went out of the world, peace was bequeathed.'
Francis Bacon.

'Peace is not an absence of war, it is a virtue, a state of mind, a disposition for benevolence, confidence, justice.'
Baruch Spinoza.

'Where there is peace, God is.'
George Herbert.

'A great many people are trying to make peace, but that has already been done. God has not left it for us to do; all we have to do is to enter into it.'
Dwight L. Moody.

Never Alone

In the **Valley** of **Death** – II

'Therefore the sisters sent to Him, saying, "Lord, behold, he whom You love is sick." When Jesus heard that, He said, "This sickness is not unto death, but for the glory of God, that the Son of God may be glorified through it." ' John 11:3, 4.

Lazarus was a friend of Jesus. One day Lazarus fell sick and word was sent to Jesus to inform him about the sickness of his friend. In other words, Mary and Martha sent word to Jesus, asking him to come to Bethany at once to attend to their brother. Van Doren states:

'What a comfort to have such a friend to whose sympathy they might appeal! – "Oh, tell thy woes to those beloved, for sorrows shared are half removed." – Though God knows all our wants, He will know them from us, and is honoured by our laying them before Him.'[1]

To their disappointment, Jesus delayed and Lazarus died. Jesus said: ' "This sickness is not unto death, but for the glory of God, that the Son of God may be glorified through it." ' It was amazing to hear those words from the mouth of Jesus. The sickness of Lazarus was not unto death and yet he died – how? Furthermore, the death of Lazarus was to glorify the Son of God. Yes, Lazarus died, but Jesus did not neglect the request of Martha and Mary. Neither did Jesus forsake his friend Lazarus in time of sickness. There are moments when we feel as though Jesus has neglected us in

Never Alone

life, but this is not so. Jesus will never ever forget his children in whatever circumstances they may find themselves, be it sickness, poverty, hunger or death. Jesus is in control of the affairs of men.

When Jesus arrived in Bethany, Martha and Mary ran to meet him with the same concern: ' "Lord, if You had been here, my brother would not have died." ' (John 11:21, 32.) Comfort and Hawley put it this way:

'In accordance with his own timetable Jesus arrived at Bethany. Martha ran out to meet him, saying, "Lord, if only you had been here." The same thought is expressed by many believers today – Lord, if you had been here, this tragedy, this accident, this disaster would not have happened! But we must forever keep in mind that he is here with us. His angels do keep watch. He knows our situation better than we know it. He has not left us nor abandoned us as orphans. He cares; he loves; he keeps.'[2]

By that time, Lazarus was already buried, but Jesus had said he was going to awaken him out of sleep (John.11: 38-44). Jesus was moved with pity to see people full of unbelief that he was able to raise Lazarus from the grave. Even his disciples did not believe it, and so Jesus wept (John 11:35) because of their unbelief. He wept because he was touched by human infirmity. Going to the tomb, he resurrected Lazarus. From this miracle we learn that when a believer dies, he is merely asleep. In the resurrection of Lazarus, we have the assurance that Jesus does not forget his faithful children who die believing in him. He will one day resurrect them to eternal life. Spence and Exell conclude: 'Divine power alone could restore Lazarus to life. All the power of men and angels would be insufficient. The same power which made man at first a living soul can alone reunite . . . at last, after the great dissolution.'[3] Death is not separation from the Infinite. In sickness and in death, God will never leave us alone. He is with us in all situations of life. It is comforting and satisfying to invest one's life in Jesus Christ who is not threatened or conquered by death.

Never Alone

John the Baptist died, but he is not forgotten. He is waiting for that beautiful resurrection morning when all those who have died in the Lord will be called to immortal life. Barclay emphasises: '. . . it matters intensely that Jesus is the Resurrection and the Life for every man who is dead in sin and dead to God today.'[4] Just as Lazarus was resurrected from death, God is able to do the same for all who trust in him. You are never alone in sickness or in death.

[1] William H. Van Doren, *Gospel of John Expository and Homiletical Commentary* (Kregel Publications), p. 917.
[2] Philip W. Comfort and Wendell C. Hawley, *Opening the Gospel of John.* (Tyndale House Publishers, Inc.), p. 182.
[3] H.D.M. Spence and Joseph S. Exell, *The Pulpit Commentary* (Wm. B. Eerdmans Publishing Company), p. 115.
[4] William Barclay, *The Gospel of John Volume 2* (The Westminster Press), p. 103.

WORDS FOR THE SICK AND SUFFERING
Never Alone
Words from Scripture

'Beloved, I wish above all things that thou mayest prosper and be in health, even as thy soul prospereth.'
3 John 1:2, KJV.

'When Jesus came into Peter's house, he saw Peter's mother-in-law lying in bed with a fever. He touched her hand and the fever left her, and she got up and began to wait on them.'
Matthew 8:14-15, NIV.

'Surely he took up our infirmities and carried our sorrows. . . .'
Isaiah 53:4.

'Is any sick among you? Let him call for the elders of the church; and let them pray over him, anointing him with oil in the name of the Lord: and the prayer of faith shall save the sick, and the Lord shall raise him up; and if he have committed sins, they shall be forgiven him. Confess your faults one to another, and pray one for another, that ye may be healed. The effectual fervent prayer of a righteous man availeth much.'
James 5:14-16, KJV.

'Jesus went throughout Galilee teaching in their synagogues, preaching the good news of the kingdom, and healing every disease and sickness among the people.' Matthew 4:23.

'When evening came, many who were demon-possessed were brought to him, and he drove out the spirits with a word and healed all the sick.'
Matthew 8:16.

Never Alone

Words from the wise

'We could never learn to be brave and patient, if there were only joy in the world.'
Helen Keller.

'They gave our Master a crown of thorns. Why do we hope for a crown of roses?'
Martin Luther.

'Afflictions are but the shadow of God's wings.'
George Macdonald.

'One who gains strength by overcoming obstacles possesses the only strength which can overcome adversity.'
Albert Schweitzer.

'Only in winter can you tell which trees are truly green. Only when the winds of adversity blow can you tell whether an individual or a country has steadfastness.'
John F. Kennedy.

'God's people have no assurances that the dark experiences of life will be held at bay, much less that God will provide some sort of running commentary on the meaning of each day's allotment of confusion, boredom, pain or achievement. It is no great matter where we are, provided we see that the Lord has placed us there, and that he is with us.'
John Newton.

Never Alone

In **Stormy** Times

'And when He had sent the multitudes away, He went up on the mountain by Himself to pray. Now when evening came, He was alone there. But the boat was now in the middle of the sea, tossed by the waves, for the wind was contrary. Now in the fourth watch of the night Jesus went to them, walking on the sea. And when the disciples saw Him walking on the sea, they were troubled, saying, "It is a ghost!" And they cried out for fear. But immediately Jesus spoke to them, saying, "Be of good cheer! It is I; do not be afraid." ' Matthew 14:23-27.

We live in a stormy world. Many are the storms that shake our faith. Storms of sickness, loneliness, distrust and fear surround us. It happened just after Jesus Christ had wrought a miracle of feeding the five thousand people with only five loaves of bread and two fish. After dispersing the people, Jesus decided to go to the mountain for prayer and meditation. Meanwhile, the disciples were commanded to get into a boat and go before him to the other side of the lake. But when the boat was far from the shore, a storm arose which threatened the disciples' lives. It is when we are far from God that the devil will find easy ground to attack us. The boat was far into the middle of the lake and Jesus Christ was far up on the mountain. Worse still, it was at night when the storm hit the boat. Sometimes the devil capitalises on opportunities that we give him when we are found in

Never Alone

avenues where we can easily fall prey to him. When we pray 'Deliver us from the evil one' (Matthew 6:13), we must put ourselves in places where God can answer our prayers.

The storm was so severe that an experienced fisherman like Simon Peter could not handle the boat. We can never overcome the trials from the devil in our human strength. The storms from the devil can be thwarted only by divine power. Storms of discouragement may come upon us, storms of fear, storms of financial perplexities, storms of disappointments, storms of despair and storms of death, but our safe anchor is only in Jesus Christ.

In the midst of this great threat, another trial appeared – a figure walking on water. The appearance threatened the disciples who thought they were seeing a ghost. The fear of the storm, coupled with the appearance of a 'ghost', further agitated their fears. In the midst of that storm, Jesus spoke and assured them, ' "Be of good cheer! It is I; do not be afraid." ' Likewise, Jesus is urging us not to despair in times of earthly storms. Rejoice, because he is in control of everything in this world, including the forces of nature. Jesus introduces himself, as 'I'. No name is mentioned. He is the one who declared to Moses ' "I AM WHO I AM." '[1] It was I who created the earth; it was I who made the barren woman, Sarah, conceive long after she had reached the menopause; it was I who made the impassable Red Sea passable; it was I who cured the incurable disease; it was I who raised Lazarus from the grave. Later he declared: It was I who ascended to heaven contrary to the science of gravity. Jesus is still saying today that he is the 'I', the One. 'There is no other name under heaven given among men by which we must be saved.'[2] 'It is I.' He did not merely introduce himself, but he comforted the disciples by saying, 'Do not be afraid.' Fear is a dangerous enemy to man. Fear can bring defeat where you are able to conquer. Christ says: Do not be afraid of anything. I am stronger than all principalities of darkness. Jesus advises: ' "And do not fear those who kill the body but cannot kill the soul. But rather fear Him who is able to

Never Alone

destroy both soul and body in hell." '

Jesus will never ignore his children who are affected by the storms of life. He will not overlook you when you are in a situation that needs divine intervention. If we cry like Peter, ' "Lord, save me!" ' (Matthew 14:30), he is quick to stretch out his hand to redeem us from every situation. Why fall into despondency when we have a Saviour who is 'able to save to the uttermost those who come to God through Him, since He ever lives to make intercession for them'[3]? After Jesus rescued Peter, who had asked Christ to make him walk on water but began to drown owing to fear, all the disciples acknowledged the power of Jesus Christ. They worshipped the Lord. Gaebelein concludes, 'The climax of the story is not the stilling of the storm (v. 32) but the confession and worship of the disciples: "Truly, you are the Son of God" (v. 33).'[4]

---

[1] Exodus 3:14.
[2] Acts 4:12.
[3] Hebrews 7:25.
[4] Frank E. Gaebelein, (ed.) *The Expositor's Bible Commentary Vol. 8* (Zondervan Publishing House), p. 345.

Never Alone

WORDS FOR THE GRIEVING

Words from Scripture

'Then shall the dust return to the earth as it was: and the spirit shall return unto God who gave it.' Ecclesiastes 12:7, KJV.

'Precious in the sight of the Lord is the death of his saints.' Psalm 116:15.

'We do not want you to be ignorant about those who fall asleep, or to grieve like the rest of men, who have no hope. We believe that Jesus died and rose again and so we believe that God will bring with Jesus those who have fallen asleep in him. According to the Lord's own word, we tell you that we who are still alive, who are left till the coming of the Lord, will certainly not precede those who have fallen asleep. For the Lord himself will come down from heaven, with a loud command, with the voice of the archangel and with the trumpet call of God, and the dead in Christ will rise first. After that, we who are still alive and are left will be caught up together with them in the clouds to meet the Lord in the air. And so we will be with the Lord for ever.' 1 Thessalonians 4:13-17.

'Christ has indeed been raised from the dead, the firstfruits of those who have fallen asleep. For since death came through a man, the resurrection of the dead comes also through a man. For as in Adam all die, so in Christ all will be made alive.' 1 Corinthians 15:20-22.

'The last enemy to be destroyed is death.' 1 Corinthians 15:26.

Never Alone

Words from the wise

'No man should be afraid to die, who hath understood what it is to live.' Thomas Fuller.

'One short sleep past, we wake eternally,
And Death shall be no more: Death, thou shalt die!' John Donne.

'Give sorrow words: the grief that does not speak Whispers the o'er fraught heart, and bids it break.' William Shakespeare, *Macbeth*.

'How sweet the name of Jesus sounds,
In a believer's ear:
It soothes his sorrows, heals his wounds,
And drives away his fear.'
John Newton.

'Earth hath no sorrow that heaven cannot heal.' Thomas Moore.

'Our trust in the Lord does not mean that there are not times of tears. I think it is a mistake as Christians to act as though trusting the Lord and tears are not compatible.'
Francis Schaeffer.

Never Alone

Look **Up**!

'When they heard these things they were cut to the heart and they gnashed at him with their teeth. But he, being full of the Holy Spirit, gazed into heaven and saw the glory of God, and Jesus standing at the right hand of God, and said, "Look! I see the heavens opened and the Son of Man standing at the right hand of God!" Then they cried out with a loud voice, stopped their ears, and ran at him with one accord; and they cast him out of the city and stoned him. And the witnesses laid down their clothes at the feet of a young man named Saul. And they stoned Stephen as he was calling on God and saying, "Lord Jesus, receive my spirit." Then he knelt down and cried out with a loud voice, "Lord, do not charge them with this sin." And when he had said this, he fell asleep.' Acts 7:54-60.

The Bible describes Stephen as 'a man full of faith and the Holy Spirit. . . . And Stephen, full of faith and power, did great wonders and signs among the people.' 'But he, being full of the Holy Spirit . . .' (Acts 6:5, 8; 7:55). Stephen was a faithful disciple and so wonders and signs accompanied his spiritual activities. During his time the word of the Lord spread to the extent that priests became obedient to the faith (Acts 6:7). Owing to jealousy, the spiritual leaders incited men to testify falsely against Stephen, saying, ' "We have heard him speak blasphemous words against Moses

Never Alone

and God." . . . They also set up false witnesses who said, "This man does not cease to speak blasphemous words against this holy place and the law." '[1] These accusations led to the death of Stephen. After he gave an address in defence of the Lord God of heaven and his deeds among people, they dragged Stephen outside the city and stoned him (Acts 7:58). They dragged him out of the city for fear of defiling the city with his blood; they feared more to defile the city than to destroy human life. The Jews had more reverence for the temple and the law than for life. It is like a person who craves for a cigarette while in church, but will not smoke within the building for fear of defiling it, forgetting that the cigarette smoke will defile his body-temple. During the stoning, Stephen did the following things in Acts 7:55-60:

Stephen gazed into heaven

Stephen knew that heaven was the throne room of the Most High God and that help would come only from him. Likewise, when we are faced with problems, we must not look to mortal man for help, but to God. Human beings do not offer solutions that satisfy, and so look up to God in times of perplexities. The Bible says: 'Set your minds on things above, not on things on the earth. For you died, and your life is hidden with Christ in God. When Christ who is our life appears, then you also will appear with Him in glory.'[2]

Stephen saw the glory of God

Those who look up to God will surely see his glory and goodness. When you look up with an eye of faith, you will not only see the clouds or stars, but the throne of God. With an eye of faith you will see Christ crucified and ready to render help to you. You will see Jesus in the Most Holy Place waiting to receive penitent sinners.

Stephen saw Jesus Christ at the right hand of God

Forty days after Jesus had overcome the devil on the

Never Alone

cross, he ascended to heaven and sat at the right hand of God. He is a Conqueror who intercedes on our behalf. All those who overcome will have a right to sit at the side of the Son of God. Our Advocate is a victor.

Stephen called on God

Stephen did not forget his source of life. Amid flying stones that were cast at him, he called on the name of God. He called on God because he had tested him and found him ready and able to help. In times of difficulties in our lives, let us call on God for wisdom and direction just as Stephen did.

Stephen committed his life to God

Stephen knew that his end had come. He decided to commit his life into the hands of Jesus, because he believed that there was life beyond the grave. He knew that by committing his life into the hands of God he was assured of the resurrection morning. He knew that Jesus had the key to the grave, and that at the trumpet sound when Jesus will appear in the clouds of heaven, he would be among the saints to rise from the grave. In times of affliction, where do you put your hope? Where is your anchor when you walk through the valley of the shadow of death? Stephen committed his life into the hands of Jesus who also committed his life into the hands of God the Father when he died on the cross (Luke 23:46). Earle explains the commitment of Stephen: '. . . that he might die as the subject of his heavenly Master – acting and suffering in the deepest submission to his divine will and permissive providence; and at the same time showing the genuine nature of the religion of his Lord, in pouring out his prayers with his blood in behalf of his murderers.'[3]

Stephen had reverence for God

When the stoning began, Stephen knelt and cried out to God. Kneeling is a sign of humility. Stephen knew that he

Never Alone

was calling upon the exalted God and he recognised God's presence with him.

Stephen interceded for his enemies

Stephen prayed to God not to charge his persecutors with the sin of stoning him because he saw the devil himself using the people to kill him. Stephen had eyes to see beyond human persecution. Stephen desired forgiveness for his enemies, which demonstrated his love for them. Marshall states:

'Then Stephen prayed for pardon for his executioners, again echoing the words of Jesus (Luke 23:34); his words stand in striking contrast to his attitude of denunciation in his speech, and illustrate how the Christian, while denouncing sin and disobedience to God in order to lead his hearers to repentance, must also have pastoral concern for them, and pray that they may be forgiven.'[4]

This is the spirit of all those who are like Christ. Jesus also prayed for his enemies, ' "Father, forgive them, for they do not know what they do." '[5]

A story is told of a wife who was married to a drunkard. Time and again she received blows from her drunken husband for apparently no reason. The wife was a Christian who persevered under tough conditions, being whipped and kicked like a ball. The moment the husband came home, his children would flee from the living-room into their bedrooms and lock themselves in. They would later hear the cry of their mother as their father took to his usual beatings. The wife, however, prayed for the husband daily until one day the husband peeped through the window and saw his wife on her knees, and he could hear her praying for him. That day brought new life to the husband. To this day he testifies that the intercessional prayer of his wife touched him. It always brings special blessings to us when we take some time to pray for those we distrust and for those who hate us.

Never Alone

Stephen fell asleep

After making things right with God and the men who were persecuting him, Stephen finally died. He slept, waiting for the day when all the sleeping saints shall rise to meet God. Those who die in the Lord are said to be asleep. The reason behind this is that when Jesus returns they will rise to everlasting life. Forgiveness is a vital lesson we learn from Stephen's life just before he died. Let us be at peace with all people while we are on earth and it will be well for us with our Father who is in heaven.

[1] Acts 6:11, 13
[2] Colossians 3:2-4.
[3] Ralph Earle, *Adam Clarke's Commentary on the Bible* (Word Publishing), p. 975.
[4] Howard Marshall, *The Tyndale New Testament. The Acts of the Apostles: An Introduction and Commentary* (William B. Eerdmans Publishing Company), p. 150.
[5] Luke 23:34.

WORDS FOR LONELY PEOPLE

Never Alone

Words from Scripture

'[God] cares for you, so cast all your anxiety on him.'
1 Peter 5:7, REB.

'Find your strength in the Lord, in his mighty power. Put on the full armour provided by God, so that you may be able to stand firm against the stratagems of the devil.'
Ephesians 6:10, 11, REB.

'The Lord is close to the broken-hearted and saves those who are crushed in spirit.'
Psalm 34:18.

' "My child, don't ignore it when the Lord disciplines you, and don't be discouraged when he corrects you. For the Lord disciplines those he loves." '
Hebrews 12:5, 6, NLT.

'The angel of the Lord encamps around those who fear him, and he delivers them.'
Psalm 34:7.

' "Set your troubled hearts at rest. Trust in God always; trust also in me. There are many dwelling-places in my Father's house. . . ." ' John 14:1, 2, REB.

'Weeping may remain for a night, but rejoicing comes in the morning.'
Psalm 30:5.

'I heard a voice thunder from the Throne: "Look! Look! God has moved into the neighbourhood, making his home with men and women! They're his people, he's their God. He'll wipe every tear from their eyes. Death is gone for good . . . all the first order of things gone. . . . Look! I'm making everything new." '
Revelation 21:3-5
(Message paraphrase.)

Never Alone
Words from the wise

'God whispers in our pleasures, shouts in our pain – but, in both, in reassuring tones, he says, "Better times are coming."'

'Do you think nobody cares what becomes of you? *God cares.* And with an infinite tenderness. He cared before you passed your care on him.'

'If you spend your whole life waiting for the storm, you will never enjoy the sunshine.'

'Worry is interest paid on trouble before it falls due.'

'Anxiety is the rust of life. Destroying its brightness and weakening its power. The antidote to anxiety is trust.'

Extracts from *God's Little Book of Encouragement*.

Never Alone

Do **Not** Fear

' "Fear not, for I am with you; Be not dismayed, for I am your God. I will strengthen you, yes, I will help you, I will uphold you with my righteous right hand." ' Isaiah 41:10.

It was in 1998 when we as a family had worship in the evening. There had been a spate of burglaries around the compound where we were staying. The previous night, our closest neighbour was badly attacked by robbers. Another neighbour had been shot dead in the presence of her children and husband, because she shouted for help after thieves took their new colour television set. Night had come and we did not know when our day of attack would be. We were all stricken with fear, not knowing when those thugs might pounce on us. Lights were switched off and we went to sleep. In the middle of the night we were awakened by a big bang from the kitchen. We jumped out of our blankets like fish hooked out of water. My wife and I both reached for our clothes in panic. I found it hard to put on my trousers because of fear. We then waited in our bedroom for our enemies to pounce on us. There was dead silence for about fifteen minutes. After that we decided to walk to the front rooms, where we found no evidence of intrusion at all. Upon careful scrutiny, we discovered that the loud bang was from a plank that had fallen to the ground. With a sigh of relief we sat down to reflect on what had happened. It was then that I

Never Alone

saw that my wife was wearing her dress inside out!

Fear knows no rank or profession. Ochs discovered:

'None of us is free from fear. There are fears from without and from within. There are fears in childhood and youth, in maturity and old age. There are fears on the land and sea and in the air. We tremble at the alarms of war, and are afraid when our financial security is taken away. Perhaps the greatest fear of all is death. There are many disquieting things in this world, the noise of which often drowns out the voice of God, who calls to us through the din, Fear not.'[1]

God has never left his children in despondency and defeat. At all times he is present to help his children. In all the problems we face, social, economical, psychological, political, spiritual and physical, Jesus is ready to assist us. It is the devil who whispers to us that God does not care about our welfare. Fear normally breaks a sound relationship.

One teenage girl had just lost her father. The father had been stricken by a stroke due to high blood pressure. After six months, the mother of that girl also fell sick. Within a week her life forces seemed to be giving way to death. The daughter visited her mother in hospital and found her condition quite unbearable. Stricken with fear of losing both parents within a period of six months, the daughter held the hand of the mother while sobbing and asked a question, 'Mum, are you going to die as well?' Fear prevents our seeing beyond the problems of this world. God our heavenly Father, who is immortal, is able to take care of us.

Ellen White insists:

'If we surrender our lives to His service, we can never be placed in a position for which God has not made provision. Whatever may be our situation, we have a Guide to direct our way; whatever our perplexities, we have a sure Counselor; whatever our sorrow, bereavement, or loneliness, we have a sympathizing Friend. If in our ignorance we make missteps, Christ does not leave us. His voice, clear and distinct, is heard saying, "I am the Way, the Truth, and the Life." John 14:6.'[2]

Never Alone

The devil's desire is to paint a dark picture of God. Ellen White also observes:

'The Lord permits trials in order that we may be cleansed from earthliness, from harsh, unchristlike traits of character. He suffers the deep waters of affliction to go over our souls in order that we may know Him and Jesus Christ whom He has sent, in order that we may have deep heart longings to be cleansed from defilement, and may come forth from the trial purer, holier, happier.'[3]

From the time man sinned, God has always been near man in order to redeem him. Even during the Exodus, God told Israel to make a sanctuary so that he could dwell among his people. God wants to be as close to you as if you were the only person in this world. In all the trials you go through, remember this song by Whittle:

> 'Dying with Jesus, by death reckoned mine,
> Living with Jesus, a new life divine,
> Looking to Jesus till glory doth shine,
> Moment by moment, O Lord, I am Thine.
>
> Refrain
>
> Moment by moment I'm kept in His love;
> Moment by moment I've life from above;
> Looking to Jesus till glory doth shine;
> Moment by moment, O Lord, I am Thine.
>
> Never a trial that He is not there,
> Never a burden that He doth not bear,
> Never a sorrow that He doth not share,
> Moment by moment I'm under His care.
>
> Never a heartache, and never a groan,
> Never a teardrop and never a moan;
> Never a danger, but there on the throne,
> Moment by moment He thinks of His own.

Never Alone

> Never a weakness that He doth not feel,
> Never a sickness that He cannot heal;
> Moment by moment, in woe or in weal,
> Jesus, my Saviour, abides with me still.'[4]

It is amazing to know that we are never alone in this world. God has not left us as orphans. We have a companion with whom we can share our burdens. Not only can he *share* our burdens, but he is also able to *bear* them all for us. Rock narrates this story:

'A friend of mine tells of how he had this lesson of the keeping power of God indelibly stamped upon his mind during a plane trip on which he encountered severe weather conditions while flying over mountainous territory. For several minutes there was a terrifying, panicky fear in the hearts of all on board as they were tossed about violently in a series of dangerous air pockets. From all indications the little plane would be shaken to pieces. This particular man, being a Christian and a minister, reached out for his Bible for reassurance. But before he could think of which text to look for in this emergency, his Bible fell open to the book of Jude, where his eyes fastened upon these words of the twenty-fourth verse, "Now unto him that is able to keep you from falling." And you, fellow traveller, when your frail bark is tossed and shaken by the stormy winds of temptation, must always remember that God is able.'[5]

God's promises in the Bible help us to cast away all fear. God promises:

'But now, thus says the Lord, who created you, O Jacob, And He who formed you, O Israel: "Fear not, for I have redeemed you; I have called you by your name; You are Mine. When you pass through the waters, I will be with you; And through the rivers, they shall not overflow you. . . . For I am the Lord your God, The Holy One of Israel, your Saviour; . . ."' [6]

Our Creator has promised to be with us. The word of God is like a torch; it gives us light. Therefore, we should not be like a man who had a torch in his hands but refused to use it at night and later fell into a ditch where a snake bit him. We

Never Alone

have all the assurance of God's ability to care for us in his word. There is nothing to fear because he is on our side as our Protector. The Bible assures us: 'Do not fear, little flock, for it is your Father's good pleasure to give you the kingdom.'[7] There is no need to fear because the One on our side is greater than any circumstance of life. All that we need to do is to trust in Jesus, our Lord and Saviour. We should not hold on to the dry branches of this world. When you hang on a dry branch, the fall is imminent and devastating. Let us hold on to Jesus Christ, who is 'able to keep you from falling'[8]. When life is unbearable, remember the promise of Jehovah: ' "I will never leave you nor forsake you." '[9] You are never alone. Indeed, never alone!

---

[1] William B. Ochs, *Glorified In Them* (Review and Herald Publishing Association), p. 73.
[2] Ellen G. White, *Christ's Object Lessons*, p. 173.
[3] *Ibid*, p. 175.
[4] Daniel W. Whittle, *The Seventh-day Adventist Hymnal* (Review and Herald Publishing Association), 507.
[5] Calvin B. Rock, *Our God is Able* (Review and Herald Publishing Association), p. 63.
[6] Isaiah 43:1-3.
[7] Luke 12:32.
[8] Jude 24.
[9] Hebrews 13:5

Never Alone

WORDS OF PROMISE

Words from Scripture

'Who dares accuse us whom God has chosen for his own? Will God? No! He is the one who has given us right standing with himself. Who then will condemn us? Will Christ Jesus? No, for he is the one who died for us and was raised to life for us and is sitting at the place of highest honour next to God, pleading for us. Can *anything* ever separate us from Christ's love?' Romans 8:33-35, NLT (emphasis ours).

'What we suffer now is nothing compared to the glory he will give us later. . . . All creation anticipates the day when it will join God's children in glorious freedom from death and decay.' Romans 8:18, 21, NLT.

'Therefore, since we have been justified through faith, we have peace with God through our Lord Jesus Christ, through whom we have gained access by faith into this grace in which we now stand.' Romans 5:1, 2.

'Therefore, there is now no condemnation for those who are in Christ Jesus.' Romans 8:1.

'God holds the high centre, he sees and sets the world's mess right. He decides what is right for us earthlings, gives people their just desserts.' Psalm 9:7, 8 (Message paraphrase).

'The Lord is my light and my salvation – whom shall I fear? The Lord is the stronghold of my life – of whom shall I be afraid?' Psalm 27:1.

Never Alone

Words from the wise

'Jesus is the yes to every promise of God.'
William Barclay.

'God's promises are like the stars; the darker the night, the brighter they shine.'
David Nicholas.

'Every promise God has ever made finds its fulfilment in Jesus.'
Joni Eareckson Tada.

'There is a living God; he has spoken in the Bible. He means what he says and will do all he has promised.' Hudson Taylor.

'The more accurately we search into the human mind, the stronger traces we everywhere find of the wisdom of him who made it.'
Edmund Burke.

'The acid test of our faith in the promises of God is never found in the easy-going, comfortable ways of life, but in the great emergencies, the times of storm and of stress, the days of adversity, when all human aid fails.' Ethel Bell.

Never Alone

Never Give Up

'So do not throw away your confidence; it will be richly rewarded.
You need to persevere so that when you have done the
will of God, you will receive what he has promised.
For in just a very little while,
"He who is coming will come and will not delay.
But my righteous one will live by faith. And if he shrinks back,
I will not be pleased with him."
But we are not of those who shrink back and are destroyed,
but of those who believe and are saved.'
Hebrews 10:35-39, NIV.

We all go through many trials in life. Hearts are bruised and broken when we lose loved ones to death. Some have gone to the grave at tender years without achieving their aspirations. Grieving parents have shed the last tear over their own children who have died. Even if we may not fully understand the reason for our suffering, we know that God one day will vindicate us. Therefore, never give up the fight for your faith. The battle is on and God will triumph. Never give up.

One day, early in the morning, I was awakened by the telephone. On answering, I heard screams of pain and grief. My neighbour had died, leaving a wife and three children. Sitting down with them on the floor, I ran out of words of comfort. It was tense, and for some moments I did not know

Never Alone

what to say and how to pray. It was a heartbreaking moment. The man I had prayed with the previous day had gone. In a few words I just prayed, 'Lord, be with your children at this tragic time and give them courage to accept the things they cannot change.' Looking at the mother, I realised she had become a widow without being prepared. I looked at the daughter who was helpless, and wailing for the dead father. Tears flowed down my cheeks. I asked the question, 'Why is it so, Lord?'

Children of God, we are indeed living in a cruel world. This cruelty all stems from the enemy of God. We are all going through pain and separation because of the calamities we face in life. Nevertheless, God is still on his throne and will always take care of his children. Never despair, never give up, and never surrender your battle of faith. He will reward our faithfulness if we do not give up. Even when we do not know the reason why we suffer, let us hold on to our faith.

In a football match, players must put in their best effort to win the game. They go through strict training; what they eat is controlled; anything that can motivate them for the game must be in place. Each day they jog and exercise to reach peak physical fitness to enable them to win a match. Finally, the lines are drawn and the game begins. One day during the Confederation of African Football, I sat in my living room watching the game. When it was just about time for the last whistle, the other team scored. There was no extra time. The scorer took the day. The losing team cried out uncontrollably. It was a painful experience, but the game was over. They wished the back liners had tightened the defence, but it was too late. The final whistle had been blown. Just as in a football match, we must be vigilant because we do not know when the Lord will come. Let us be faithful to the point of death. Let us fight on until we have overcome. The battle is still on. Let us fight on, saints, because the great controversy between good and evil rages and it is almost over. The signs of Jesus' coming point to the

Never Alone

imminence of that long-awaited event; never give up.

A young man had fallen in love with a young lady and their courtship was going well. Parents and friends were looking forward to the couple getting married. Then the young man received a letter indicating that his fiancée had decided to break off the relationship. Upon further investigation, he discovered that his close friend had fallen in love with his girlfriend. Traumatised and disillusioned with the whole matter, he decided to commit suicide. He got a rope and tied it to a dry branch. He made a knot and pushed his head through the loop to take his own life. In the process of his struggling, the branch broke and he fell to the ground. He never again tried to end his life. Yes, there are moments when we go into despair and disappointment. Sometimes our close friends cause us unhappiness. Even when it is so painful, let us not give up. Let us look to God for help for he will not let us down. We are never alone. We must never give up our faith and lose our commitment to God simply because the road is rough. Sometimes those we hold dear to us may disappoint us. Our spouses, neighbours, workmates, relatives, may sometimes disturb our peace, but God will never forsake his own. Therefore, we must not give up trusting in God. He is not man that he can change his mind. He is a Friend in need and in deed. Circumstances and situations may change on our side, but God's love and care will never change. For this reason, don't let us give up our faith in him.

In athletics, what counts most is not how many kilometres you have run, but when you cross the finishing line. The athlete should endeavour to run all the way until he comes to the tape. This is when he is considered a winner. Even in our Christian faith, we are compared to athletes who are fighting for a prize. They go through a lot of training and lessons in self-control so that they are fit for the competition. In the end, only one gets the first prize. But when it comes to eternal life, God has promised the reward to all those who overcome. It is not just for the star athlete, but for all who

Never Alone

believe in God and have stood fast to the end. The Bible says: 'He who endures to the end shall be saved.' (Matthew 24:13.) It is not how much you have attended church services and participated in holy ordinances, but how fully you have trusted in God. In our Christian faith, we are admonished not to give up. We must hold on to our faith until Jesus comes. We need to persevere in our commitment to God. Especially when trials buffet us, we must look up to him for direction.

Jesus Christ tells us not to look behind as Mrs Lot did. He says, ' "Remember Lot's wife." ' (Luke 17:32.) Why should we remember Lot's wife? What was special about her? There were many married ladies during Jesus' time. We have to remember Lot's wife because of the way she missed her eternal reward. She despised the counsel of God by looking back to Sodom and Gomorrah. Consider the following:

She was escorted by angels out of Sodom. The hands of angels took the hands of Lot's wife and yet she defied the instruction and looked back to Sodom. She had the privilege of mingling with angels. She even touched the hand of the angel but considered it nothing special.

Her body was in the plains while her heart was in Sodom. To begin with, she ran, covering quite a distance from the city to flee for her life in the company of her husband and two daughters. Yet, even though she was running away from the city, her heart was still in Sodom. It was difficult for her to continue in the race as she recalled the wealth she had amassed and the pleasures of Sodom, and she finally decided to give up. In looking back, she actually distrusted God. She'd despised the admonition. She'd felt compelled to leave Sodom contrary to her personal inclination. She gave up her salvation in preference to the pleasures of the world. In a moment she turned into a pillar of salt. There are many who are in the church but lack that individual commitment to and relationship with God. She ran a few kilometres out of the danger zone but did not reach her destination.

Never Alone

Four left Sodom but three reached their destination. They were four in number, that is, Lot, Mrs Lot and the two daughters. There are many people who go to church and out of these massive groups there are some who are like Lot's wife, just following others. And there are some who love their God and are willing to grasp the grace of Jesus. To accept or reject salvation is an individual decision. The faith of our parents or sisters will not count on that judgement day. We have to make our own commitment to God. Hence Jesus reminds us of how Lot's wife gave up her faith in preference to worldly pleasures. She died and has gone into oblivion. The lesson we get from this is that we must never give up. Temporal pleasures deceive. Don't settle for temporal gains. Look up to what is stored for you in heaven. Never give up your faith because of what you can see with the naked eye. God has provided many and better things in eternity. Four left Sodom but only three reached their destination.

Never give up your faith in God because of pressing earthly things which are perishable. We are to lay up our treasures in heaven where there is no decay or corruption (Matthew 6:19-21). There are times when we incur losses in our business and even suffer the loss of a family. Even in such situations, never give up your faith but keep trusting in God. When you are hit in all ways and the future seems dim and dark, look to God for help.

I grew up in a village. Early in the morning we would yoke the oxen to go into the fields to plough. When you are holding the plough, you must not lose focus and attention. You must put the plough in position so that you cut the earth accordingly. In the same manner, we must never lose focus on our Saviour, regardless of many inviting attractions. Focus on Jesus. Ignore the negatives and dwell on the positives in life.

We are living in a world of sickness. Some have suffered at the hands of the enemy for many years. Some will go through loss of jobs on account of their faith; some will face

Never Alone

disappointment from their closest ones; yet others will bemoan their bachelorhood or spinsterhood. To such I say, 'Hold on; never give up. Continue trusting in God.' Some have lost their vehicles at gunpoint. Some have lost their whole family in a plane crash. Some have left their homes and never come back; but, child of God, never give up your faith. Wait for God to wipe away your tears on that day when he comes to redeem us from this earth. We should not look back after we have accepted Jesus. We need to press on until Jesus comes or up to the point of death. The reward is there for those who persevere in the faith. No matter what problem you might face, just stand up for Jesus, and never give up.

Never Alone

Words
that contrast our thinking with God's thinking

Our thinking	God's thinking
'It's impossible.'	'All things are possible.' Luke 18:27.
'I'm too tired.'	'I will give you rest.' Matthew 11:28-30.
'Nobody loves me.'	'I love you.' John 3:16; 13:34.
'I can't go on.'	'My grace is sufficient.' 2 Corinthians 12:9.
'I can't work things out.'	'I will direct your steps.' Proverbs 3:5, 6.

Never Alone

Our thinking	God's thinking
'I can't do it.'	'You can do all things.' Philippians 4:13.
'I can't do it.'	'I am able.' 2 Corinthians 9:8.
'I can't forgive myself.'	'I forgive you.' 1 John 1:9; Romans 8:1.
'I can't manage.'	'I will supply all your needs.' Philippians 4:19.
'I am scared!'	'I have not given you a spirit of fear.' 2 Timothy 1:7.
'I am worried and frustrated.'	'Cast all your cares on me.' 1 Peter 5:7.

Never Alone

Our Father

> 'This is how you should pray:
> "Our Father in heaven, hallowed be your name. . . ." '
> Matthew 6:9, NIV.

The name 'father' is sweet to hear. It denotes protection. The father has a responsibility to protect the family from outside forces that tamper with the peace at home. His role is unique. He creates an environment where the children will be defended from their enemies. In my village, all that I knew was that my father was the strongest man. No one could ever beat him or push him around. It was my belief that my father would not die but live forever. If any person tampered with me and I reported him to my father, then I knew that I was protected. Unfortunately, my father met his fate and died. But praise be to God; our Heavenly Father lives forever.

The name father also denotes a provider. The father's role is to provide necessities for the family. He must go to work and bring food; he must go hunting and bring some game meat. He has to ensure that a child is educated, fed, clothed, receives medical care, etc. The father as a provider must sacrifice his life to fend for the family at whatever cost. He must ensure that food is available.

The name father also denotes leadership. He must guide the family in activities that will bring them prosperity. The

Never Alone

father is the family's role model. The commitment and hard work of the children are unlikely to rise above those of the father. The father should set the example in speech, dress, respect, etc. Children will surely copy the way the father talks or laughs. Father is a name that gives assurance to society. When a father behaves in a demeaning manner, that is what the children are likely to copy. The father must stand out as a role model in everything. However, some fathers have acted as bad examples. Some have betrayed their families. Some have not provided for their children's needs, but our Heavenly Father is there for us when our earthly fathers fail us. We have heard of fathers who have sexually and emotionally abused their own children, but our Heavenly Father, who sees all, will bring them into judgement (Matthew 18:6, 10).

The disciples came to Jesus to ask him to teach them how to pray. Without any hesitation, Jesus responded and said, pray thus: 'Our Father. . . .' From the opening of the Lord's Prayer, we find an all-encompassing address. Our Father reflects the fact that he is the God of all people, of every kindred and tongue. He is a Father to the poor and rich; he is a Father to the orphans, he is a Shepherd to those without protection. God is for all classes of people. The godly and the infidel were both created by him. He is our Father, regardless of how far we have fallen short of his glory. He is worthy to be our Father because he does not change. As he was yesterday, so he will be today, tomorrow, and forevermore. He is a Father to you as a widow, widower, or orphan.

Therefore, regardless of hard times you may go through, just know that God is a Father who cares for you. Some people feel God cares only for them, but he is a Father to all who need his hand of protection. He is a Father who dwells in heaven. Earthly residences may change, but our Father is in heaven where there is no corruption and we need no appointments to meet him.

Our Father in heaven oversees the affairs of men and

Never Alone

provides for their daily needs. He is the one who sets seasons and provides for humankind. He controls the galaxies and puts things in their order. Your Father knows what you need. He asks you only to do your part by praying and asking him to open the windows of blessing for your daily needs. We need not live like orphans. Yes, we might have lost our earthly father, but we have a Father in heaven who will never slumber or die. He is always alive to intercede for us. Our Father is in control of this universe, so do not worry, child of God. You have a Father who does not ignore your smallest concerns. He always looks at you with keen interest and longs to redeem his own child from the miry clay of disappointments and disillusionment. He stands ready with his arms outstretched to you to receive all your cares. Cheer up! You have a Father who will not overlook your personal needs. Trust him and honour him in your life and he will surely lead you into the paths of peace and everlasting joy.

Never Alone

Words for seekers

'He is able also to save them to the uttermost that come unto God by him.' Hebrews 7:25, KJV.

'Anyone, any place, any time, who comes to Jesus is always, always, *always* accepted. He saves to the uttermost and the outermost.'

'I will heal their waywardness and love them freely, for my anger has turned away from them.' Hosea 14:4.

'There is a way back to the Father's house for every prodigal son and daughter no matter how "backslidden" they may consider themselves to be.'

'See, I have placed before you an open door that no-one can shut.' Revelation 3:8.

'God sees to it that the door of opportunity is always open for the Christian. If one door closes it is because another is about to open.'

'We may tire, grow weary, stumble and fall, but if we depend on the Lord for strength we may yet soar.'

'Those who hope in the Lord will renew their strength. They will soar on wings like eagles; they will run and not grow weary, they will walk and not be faint.' Isaiah 40:31.

Never Alone

Words for seekers

'Can a mother forget the baby at her breast and have no compassion on the child she has borne? Though she may forget, I will not forget you! See, I have engraved you on the palms of my hands.' Isaiah 49:15, 16.

'God's love and compassion for you are fiercer, even, than those of a mother for a newborn baby.'

'Be strong and courageous. Do not be terrified; do not be discouraged, for the Lord your God will be with you wherever you go.' Joshua 1:9.

'If you ask for his presence, God is prepared to be your forever Companion – wherever you go, at all times.'

'God is not unjust; he will not forget your work and the love you have shown him as you have helped his people and continue to help them.' Hebrews 6:10.

'God is no one's debtor. He will make it up to you.'

'I will repay you for the years the locusts have eaten.' Joel 2:25.

'It has been said, "You cannot kill time without injuring eternity." However, when we return to God, he has a way of making up the wasted years. . . .'

Never Alone

It is **Over**

'Then I saw a new heaven and a new earth, for the first heaven and the first earth had passed away, and there was no longer any sea. I saw the Holy City, the New Jerusalem, coming down out of heaven from God, prepared as a bride beautifully dressed for her husband. And I heard a loud voice from the throne saying, "Now the dwelling of God is with men, and he will live with them. They will be his people, and God himself will be with them and be their God. He will wipe every tear from their eyes. There will be no more death or mourning or crying or pain, for the old order of things has passed away." ' Revelation 21:1-4, NIV.

We are living in this world of much suffering and pain. Hardly a day passes by without our seeing the marks of pain and grief. In the above passage of Scripture, we find peace and joy. John, the apostle of God, is taken in a vision where he sees the new order of things on earth. He is shown by God how the redeemed will live and inherit the earth. The home of the saved has come down from heaven and the saints are with God.

Jesus is coming again. The Bible succinctly states that Jesus is coming again. He has promised in his Word that he will come to take his children home. The psalmist reveals: 'Our God comes and will not be silent; a fire devours before him, and around him a tempest rages. He summons the heavens above, and the earth, that he may judge his

Never Alone

people: "Gather to me my consecrated ones, who made a covenant with me by sacrifice." ' (Psalm 50:3-5, NIV.) Our God is not ignorant of the situation here on earth. He is aware of the afflictions of his chosen ones. However, God will not be silent forever. He is going to intervene and set things right, but he is waiting for you and me to repent. Even if we do not repent, God, according to his promise, will surely come. And when he comes, he will descend with great authority to claim his people, saying, ' "Gather to me my consecrated ones, who made a covenant with me by sacrifice." ' Accepting Jesus Christ as a personal Saviour requires sacrifice and self-denial. Those who are sacrificing for Jesus' sake will get their reward.

In comforting his disciples Jesus said, ' "Do not let your hearts be troubled. Trust in God; trust also in me. In my Father's house are many rooms; if it were not so, I would have told you. I am going there to prepare a place for you. And if I go and prepare a place for you, I will come back and take you to be with me that you also may be where I am." ' (John 14:1-3, NIV.) They had enjoyed peace and comfort with the Lord. But the time had come when Jesus was about to return to his Father after his death. And so Jesus entreats them not to be troubled. In one way or another we all come to a point when our hearts are troubled. When we face up to the difficulties of this life, we are definitely troubled; but Jesus is urging us to trust in God. This is unwavering trust. In pain or joy we ought to depend on God. In sickness and death we need to trust God and his Word. He has gone to prepare a place for those who trust him and solely depend on him. He himself said, 'I will come again', and we are all looking forward to that great day.

When Jesus comes, there will be two groups of people, those who have rejected his grace of free salvation and those who have accepted him as a personal Saviour. Those who reject him now will never be given a second chance at his Second Coming. We are to prepare to meet him now, *today*. We are to choose him as the Lord of our lives. On the

Never Alone

other hand, those who trust him will rejoice when he comes again. Pay-day is coming when we shall be rewarded according to our works.

Coming back to our key text, we read that John saw a new heaven and a new earth. This scenario is about the home of the saved. The saints have now inherited the land God has prepared for them. The old earth, full of hailstorms, diseases, suffering, earthquakes, tornadoes, floods, and carnivorous animals has gone. The old order of things is removed when Jesus comes again.

The apostle John continues with his description of the Holy City where sin no longer abides. He sees a place where there will be no more security guards and gadgets to protect our properties. No more walls or fences around us, because the city is holy and the inhabitants are holy, and their thoughts and deeds are holy. There will be no more policemen and security men because the inhabitants are at peace with one another and have integrity. This Holy City is not made by human hands; the planner and builder is God. It is not coming from the earth but from heaven. The City is beautiful and John compares it to a bride adorned for her husband.

As John views the Holy City, he hears a voice from the throne of God, 'Now the dwelling of God is with men' (v. 3). In that City, we shall not be lonely. Our Lord and Saviour, Immanuel, meaning 'God with us', will be in our midst. If God will live among us it must be a really wonderful place. It is up to us to make a choice to live with our Saviour forever. Since God will be with us, there will be no troubles among us. When Jesus was with the disciples he fed the hungry, raised the dead, healed the sick, calmed the tempestuous storms, walked on water, cleansed the incurable disease leprosy and performed many other miracles. From his past works, we can be assured that God will protect us as he will be living among us. We shall be privileged to interact with him. It will not be a boring place, but an exciting one. We cannot explain the beauty of the new earth and new heaven.

Never Alone

No pen can describe the joy of the saints. No story-teller can adequately portray the peace there. We must decide *now* to be there and see for ourselves. John the apostle saw just a miniature of the whole City.

The exciting thing about the saved is that, 'He will wipe every tear from their eyes. There will be no more death or mourning or crying or pain, for the old order of things has passed away.' (Revelation 21:4.) Crying and mourning is the order of life here on earth. There is no peace. Family members are going through grief. There is crying in the economic world for better pay. There is crying for justice in the land today. The innocent sometimes suffer imprisonment while the guilty are set free. Those who work hard end up getting little pay. Suffering and crying is the way of life in this earth today. Spouses wet their pillows with tears. Many are crying for help when help is nowhere to be found. The hungry are crying for food when the rich are dying of overeating. The poor are crying for relief while the affluent are enjoying their investments. We are indeed in a world of crying. But when Jesus comes again, there will be no crying because our Father will be among us and he will provide us with everything we need.

There will be no more death or mourning or pain when Jesus comes. The order of life today is such that we are inflicted with the pain of death. Every family on earth has experienced the pain of separation. Whether we are godly or not, we all suffer the pain of death and mourning. Old and young people alike are dying today. Every day in Africa, the mortuary is receiving a corpse. Every day physicians are writing death certificates. Every day, somewhere, someone is laid in the grave. Someone today is buying a coffin for a loved one. It is a world of suffering. However, the only hope for the troubled world is in Jesus coming again to set up a new kingdom of peace. Yes, in that new home there will be no dark valley, no more pain and sorrow. Eternal peace will reign in our hearts and in the universe.

When Jesus comes, we shall see our beloved ones who

Never Alone

died in Jesus, and they will be with us if we have remained faithful. There will be a great reunion and great joy. Imagine a mother seeing her children again in heaven. Imagine walking side by side with your life's partner! Imagine seeing your best friend there and sharing a walk on the green carpet of grass. The day is coming when this will be a reality. A day of rejoicing and restoration, a day of redemption and restitution, a day of eternal bliss is coming. Therefore, child of God, plan to be there. Don't wait and miss this chance. All that you have to do is to accept Jesus as your Lord and Saviour. When Jesus comes, there will be no more pain, no more dying, no more stealing, no more sexual abuse, no more rape cases, no more guns, no more surgical operations, no more robberies, no more fires, no more volcanoes, and no more earthquakes. These things will be over. Suffering will be over when Jesus comes. Satan will be no more. We shall be with Jesus forever and ever. We shall never be alone because Jesus will be among us.

Never Alone

Prayer
and perseverance

'O God, give me the gift of perseverance.
If I fail in something the first time,
help me to try and try again, until I succeed.
If I have to do something difficult, help me not to get
discouraged, but to keep on trying.
If I find that results are slow to come,
give me patience that I may learn to wait.
Help me to remember that the more difficult a thing is,
the greater is the satisfaction in achieving it.
Help me to welcome every difficulty as a
challenge and an opportunity for victory;
through Jesus Christ my Lord. Amen.'
William Barclay.

Never Alone

'O Holy Spirit,
give me faith that will protect me
from despair, from passions, and from vice;
Give me such love for God and men
as will blot out all hatred and bitterness;
Give me the hope that will deliver me
From fear and faintheartedness.
O holy and merciful God
my Creator and Redeemer,
my Judge and Saviour,
you know me and all that I do.
You hate and punish evil with no respect of persons;
You forgive the sins of those
who sincerely pray for forgiveness,
you love goodness, and reward it with a clear conscience,
and, in the world to come,
with a crown of righteousness.
I remember in your presence all my loved ones,
my fellow prisoners, on all who in this house
perform their hard service;
Lord, have mercy.
restore me to liberty
and enable me to live now
that I may answer before you and before men.
Lord, whatever this day may bring,
your name be praised. Amen.'
Dietrich Bonhoeffer (prayed on the day of his execution).

Never Alone
Words of blessing

'May the Lord bless you and take care of you;
may the Lord be kind and gracious to you;
may the Lord look on you with favour and give you peace.'
From Numbers chapter 6.

'The grace of the Lord Jesus Christ, the love of God and the fellowship of the Holy Spirit be with you all.'
2 Corinthians 13:14.

'The peace of God, which passeth all understanding, keep your hearts and minds in the knowledge and love of God, and of his Son, Jesus Christ our Lord; and the blessing of God Almighty, the Father, the Son and the Holy Spirit, be amongst you and remain with you always. Amen.'
Anglican Prayer Book

'God be in my head, and in my understanding;
God be in my eyes, and in my looking;
God be in my mouth, and in my speaking;
God be in my heart, and in my thinking;
God be at my end and at my departing.'
From a *Book of Hours* (1514).

'The Lord Jesus Christ be near to defend thee, within thee to refresh thee, around thee to preserve thee, before thee to guide thee, behind thee to justify thee, above thee to bless thee; who liveth and reigneth with the Father and the Holy Spirit, God forevermore.'
Author unknown (tenth century).

Never Alone

Words of prayer for the dying

'Gentle and mysterious God,
you gave me the gift of life,
and will be with me at my death;
I am afraid of dying suddenly,
violently or painfully,
and I dread leaving behind those I love.
I give you my fears, as a gift of trust in you.
Help me to face the truth that we are all dying,
and let me remember
that if I can face up to my mortality with honesty,
I can live more fully now.'
Angela Ashwin.

'Into your hands, O Lord, I commit my spirit.' Psalm 31:5.

'Bring us, O Lord, at our last awakening
into the house and gate of heaven,
to enter into that gate and dwell in that house
where shall be no darkness nor dazzling,
but one equal light;
no noise nor silence, but one equal music;
no fears nor hopes, but one equal possession;
no ends nor beginnings, but one equal eternity
in the habitations of your glory and dominion,
world without end.'
John Donne.

Never Alone

Words of prayer on bereavement

'My God
why have you let this happen?
why did you forsake us?
Creator – why uncreate?
Redeemer – why destroy wholeness?
Source of love – why rip away
the one I loved so utterly?
Why, why, O God?

In this pit of darkness
hollowed out by grief and screaming,
I reach out to the one I loved
and cannot touch.
Where are you, God?
Where are you?
Except here
in my wounds
Which are also yours?
God,
as I hurl at you
my aching rage and bitterness,
hold me,
and stay here
until this hacked-off stump of my life
discovers greenness again.'
Angela Ashwin.

Never Alone

Prayer for use by those who will be laying hands on others:

> 'And now, O God, I give myself to you,
> Empty me of all that is not of you,
> Cleanse me from all unrighteousness
> And, according to your will,
> Take my hands and use them for your glory.'
> Dorothy Kerin.

Prayer for healing:

> 'May the healing power of our risen Lord Jesus Christ fill your whole being, body, mind and spirit. May he take away all that hurts or harms you, and give you his peace.'
> Author unknown.

Prayer for the sick:

> 'May the light of God surround you,
> the presence of God enfold you,
> and the power of God heal you,
> today and always.'
> Angela Ashwin.

Never Alone

Words
of care for the sick and their carers

'Jesus our Healer,
we place in your gentle hands those who are sick.
Ease their pain,
and heal the damage done to them
in body, mind or spirit.
Be present to them through the support of their friends
and in the care of doctors and nurses,
and fill them with the warmth of your love
now and always. Amen.'
Angela Ashwin.

Never Alone

'Living God, Source of light and life,
we come to you as broken members of your body;
your strength is our strength,
your health is our health,
and your being is our being.
Grant us your wisdom in our work,
your love in our pain,
and your peace in our heart.
Send your blessing on all those who care for the sick,
and those whom they serve,
and give us the joy of everlasting love.
In the name of Jesus your Son.'
Adapted.

Never Alone Bibliography

Anderson, Roy Allan. *Unfolding Daniel's Prophecies*. Pacific Press Publishing Association.

Barclay, William. *The Gospel of John Volume 2*. The Westminster Press.

Branson, William Henry. *Drama of the Ages*. Southern Publishing Association.

Comfort, Philip W. and Hawley, Wendell C. *Opening the Gospel of John*. Tyndale House Publishers, Inc.

Dybdahl, John L. *The Abundant Life Bible Amplifier: Exodus*. Pacific Press Publishing Association.

Earle, Ralph. *Adam Clarke's Commentary on the Bible*. Word Publishers.

Gaebelein, Frank E. *The Expositor's Bible Commentary Vol. 8*. Zondervan Publishing House.

Hawthorne, Gerald F. *The Presence & Power*. Word Publishing.

The Holy Bible, *New King James Version*.

Kennedy, John. *The Book of Daniel from the Christian Standpoint*. Eyre and Spottiswoode.

Maxwell, Mervyn C. *God Cares Vol. 1*. Pacific Press Publishing Association.

Ochs, William B. *Glorified In Them*. Review and Herald Publishing Association.

Shea, William, H. *The Abundant Life Bible Amplifier: Daniel 1-7*. Pacific Press Publishing Association.

Smith, Uriah. *Daniel and the Revelation*. Southern Publishing Association.

Spence, H. D. M. and Exell, Joseph S. *The Pulpit Commentary Vol. 17 Gospel of John*. Wm. B. Eerdmans Publishing Company.

Marshall, Howard. *The Tyndale New Testament. The Acts of the Apostles: An Introduction and Commentary*. William B. Eerdmans Publishing Company.

Rock, Calvin B. *Our God is Able*. Review and Herald Publishing Association.

Van Doren, William H. *Gospel of John Expository and*

Homiletical Commentary. Kregel Publications.

White, Ellen G. *Christ's Object Lessons.* Review and Herald Publishing Association.

White, Ellen G. *The Desire of Ages.* Pacific Press Publishing Association.

White, Ellen G. *Education.* Pacific Press Publishing Association.

Whittle, Daniel W. *The Seventh-day Adventist Hymnal.* Review and Herald Publishing Association.